SEEKING HAPPINESS

RE-ENERGIZING MY MIND

T. Kripalu

Copyright © 2020 by: T. Kripalu

All rights reserved.

ISBN: 9798579157980

SEEKING HAPPINESS
RE-ENERGIZING MY MIND

Copyright © by **T. Kripalu 2020.** All rights reserved. Printed in the United States of America. No part of this book may be used or reproduced in any manner whatsoever without written permission except in the case of brief quotations embodied in critical articles and reviews. For more information about the ideas discussed in this book, please contact The Angel Wing, LLC at: TheAngelWing19@gmail.com

WEBSITE

www.TheAngelWing.com

To order additional copies of this book, please visit:

Amazon.com

or contact The Angel Wing, LLC at:

E-Mail: TheAngelWing19@gmail.com
302-283-9878

Please leave your name and phone number and the author will contact you. You may also send text messages.

Published by: T. Kripalu
Distributed by: Kindle Direct Publishing

I extend my sincere welcome to all readers and express my heartfelt appreciation to all those who are taking their valuable time to read this book. May my journey in life serve as an inspiration to young and old, in all walks of life, to <u>never</u> give up and <u>recognize</u> that immense raw personal power can be awakened by re-energizing one's mind, changing perspectives, and serving humanity.

THE HAPPINESS WE ALL SEEK IS HIDDEN WITHIN US, JUST WAITING TO BE NATURALLY DISCOVERED.

DEDICATION

Dedicated to my dearest wife Ammani, for the love and affection I received over our 49 plus years of our marriage.

TABLE TO CONTENTS

ACKNOWLEDGMENTS
Page: XI

FOREWORD
Pages: XII - XV

PREFACE
Pages: 1 - 2

PART 1

CHAPTER 1
THE FORMATIVE YEARS – A MEDLEY OF EMOTIONS
Pages: 5 - 9

CHAPTER 2
REACHING FOR THE STARS (AND GETTING IT!!) – AMBITION, HOPE AND SUCCESS
Pages: 10 - 12

CHAPTER 3
MY LIFE AT THE MILITARY ACADEMY – OVERCOMING CHALLENGES
Pages: 13 - 24

CHAPTER 4
LIFE AS AN OFFICER – PART 1 – THE TRAVAILS AND TURMOIL OF ARMY LIFE
Pages: 25 - 30

CHAPTER 5
LIFE ABROAD AS AN INDIAN ARMY OFFICER
Pages: 31 - 32

CHAPTER 6
BACK IN INDIA
Pages: 33 - 38

CHAPTER 7
POST-ARMY CAREER
Pages: 39 - 42

CHAPTER 8
ACTIVE RETIREMENT
Pages: 43 - 54

PART 2

CHAPTER 9
TRANSFORMATION: DEALING WITH CATASTROPHES, AND CRISES
Pages: 57 - 60

PICTURES
Pages: 61 - 106

CHAPTER 10
THE DAILY PRACTICES THAT GIVE HAPPINESS
Pages: 107 - 108

CHAPTER 11
SEEKING HAPPINESS THROUGH GIVING
Pages: 109 - 110

CHAPTER 12
EXPECTATIONS FROM OTHERS, INDEPENDENCE, AND HAPPINESS
Pages: 111 - 112

CHAPTER 13
SEEKING HAPPINESS THROUGH RELATIONSHIPS
Pages: 113 - 114

CHAPTER 14
SEEKING HAPPINESS THROUGH A SPIRITUAL QUEST
Pages: 115 - 116

CHAPTER 15
MEDITATION AND HAPPINESS
Pages: 117 - 120

CHAPTER 16
THE WISDOM IN SAYINGS AND QUOTATIONS
Pages: 121 - 124

CHAPTER 17
PRACTICAL MATTERS AND TRAITS THAT LEAD TO HAPPINESS
Pages: 125 - 138

CHAPTER 18
INDIVIDUALS AND FAMILIES WHO HAVE CONTRIBUTED TO MY HAPPINESS
Pages: 139 - 144

CHAPTER 19
SELF -DISPOSSESSION AND GIVING TO OTHERS AS A CONDUIT FOR HAPPINESS AND SATISFACTION
Pages: 145 - 150

CHAPTER 20
SELF-RELIANCE IS AN ESSENTIAL INGREDIENT OF HAPPINESS
Pages: 151 - 154

CHAPTER 21
EGO IS THE NEMESIS OF HAPPINESS
Pages: 155 - 156

CHAPTER 22
BRAIN GAMES AND KEEPING MYSELF MENTALLY ACTIVE – EXAMPLE OF SUDOKU
Pages: 157 - 160

CHAPTER 23
DO NOT FIGHT TECHNOLOGY, EMBRACE IT – USE IT TO YOUR ADVANTAGE!! *KEEP LEARNING*
Pages: 161 - 162

CHAPTER 24
THE MIND IS MORE POWERFUL THAN THE BODY – A STORY OF DISCIPLINE AND DETERMINATION
Pages: 163 - 168

CHAPTER 25
THE TRANSFORMATION OF MY LIFE – *LEAD ME FROM DARKNESS TO LIGHT, FROM IGNORANCE TO KNOWLEDGE, FROM MORTALITY TO IMMORTALITY*
Pages: 169 - 180

CHAPTER 26
THE PANDEMIC OF OUR TIMES: CORONA VIRUS—COVID 19
Pages: 181 - 186

CHAPTER 27
SILENCE
Pages: 187 - 192

EPILOGUE
Pages: 193 - 195

APPENDIX A
INSPIRATIONAL THOUGHTS FOR FURTHER CONTEMPLATION
Pages: 169 - 198

TESTIMONIALS
Pages: 199 - 205

ACKNOWLEDGMENTS

This book would never have happened without the inspiration from my dear nephew, Bin Srinidhi and his wife Devi. Their motivation is what made me hand write 250 pages and encouraged me to go down memory lane and reminisce about the wonderful years of my life. Apart from the inspiration, Nidhi has also worked tirelessly to give shape and structure to my work. Making it not just more meaningful but also instructional in some ways. Additionally, Sridhar Reddy created all the hand drawn sketches for this book, and I express my gratitude for his hard work and affection. Finally, Sachin has done a lot of the heavy lifting during the last mile to make this a reality - from the final edits, to putting it together, to getting it published both on and offline. Thank you, dear Nidhi, dear Devi and dear Sachin. I could never have done it without you all! Thanks also to my dear sons, Anand and Vinny for chipping in. Nothing in my life is complete without the two of you.

FOREWORD

I consider it a distinct honor and a great privilege to be asked to introduce a remarkable man who has written an amazing book!! The author is my beloved uncle Kripalu, known as *"uncle,"* to all my friends and relatives. No one who has met him for even a few minutes could forget him. Almost all of them cherish the memory of uncle's all-embracing charm and love, his engaging stories, and his experiences in life that speak to a life of amazing transformation.

Born to a poor family struggling for survival in an obscure corner of highly conservative and religious pre-independent India, Kripalu uncle has, over the ninety-four years of his life, transformed himself in many ways. His indomitable will and determination, combined with an ability for adventure and bold initiatives, enabled him to get into the prestigious defense academy of the Indian army and become a distinguished officer in the army. Overcoming challenges that would have been deemed unsurmountable by most others, he achieved great success and finally retired as a brigadier. Physically, with extraordinary discipline, he transformed himself from a half-starved weakling to a strong, muscular, and active officer in the army and continues to be one of the fittest persons I have come across, even at the age of ninety-four. Academically, he has continuously sought to acquire knowledge and starting from being the only non-graduate candidate to enter the academy in his batch, has acquired a graduate degree in management studies. Intellectually, he has transformed himself through introspection and reflection to one of the wisest persons I am associated with. Spiritually, as he describes in this book, he has transformed himself from an angry young person to one of the most loving, generous, and compassionate persons, full of serenity and at peace with himself and the world. Indeed, his has been a life of amazing transformations.

As he weaves his life-story into this narrative about transformation and re-engineering of his mind to become a happier and wise person, he provides the tools and mechanisms that we can use to transform our lives as well. I am blessed to have been associated with him for a long time. With every interaction with him, I have learned how to make my own life more purposeful and happier. As such, I consider him to be my mentor, teacher, friend, philosopher, and guide. He has the extraordinary ability to provide guidance like a father, with the love and tenderness of a mother.

I cannot but feel a sense of immense gratitude for being able to read the book and learn to become a better person.

As I read this book, I realize the secret to happiness in two different dimensions. First, he provides a conceptual framework for achieving happiness. In this, his advice echoes those offered by scriptures of many religions, by the philosophers of yore, and by the modern educators who run courses on the psychology of happiness. But where this book provides a distinctive edge, is in providing practical guidance to the process of seeking happiness. How does one modify one's behavior during interactions with close family members like the spouse, children, and parents? How does one deal with fears and anxieties that come with uncertainties? How does one convert grief and sorrow into opportunities? He draws on his rich experience in life to provide practical solutions that are relevant to modern times. In this, he connects the wisdom of the scriptures to the practicality of daily life. It is a book that is sorely needed to heal the ravages of the modern-day stress of everyday life on human happiness, particularly in these challenging times as we battle a raging pandemic.

We live in a world of unprecedented wealth, and abundant resources to provide us with material comfort, and an amazingly rapid growth of technology that provides access to unlimited knowledge within the reach of almost every person. The opportunities for improvement and learning are almost limitless. If happiness resulted from material comforts, these advances should have led to a utopia with happy individuals, living in a world of peaceful and loving coexistence. Yet, the world is tearing itself apart with polarizing religious, political, and economic ideologies, untold cruelty and suffering, and suppression of the basic rights of many fellow human beings. The technology is often wantonly used destructively to impose pain on others and exploit the only inhabitable planet that we know. More insidiously and unintentionally, the technology powerhouses have, in their quest for profits, invaded our privacy and use customized technology to selectively guide our access to information, thereby molding our behavior to profit them. We live at a time when mental health problems are increasing, suicides among young people are more common than ever, and group responsibility is at its nadir. Freedom of the individual is mistaken for reckless disregard for others and we have created a self-centered, uncaring, and unloving world with little value of human life and little care for human suffering. Individuals are exposed to a daily narrative of crimes and cruelty that makes them fearful and anxious. The younger generation is increasingly addicted to their devices and content that manipulate their behavior to seek constant social recognition that suits corporate interests rather than foster growth, responsibility and empathy towards others. Suffice it to say, the advances in science and technology and the extraordinary distribution of knowledge, have not been able to produce happier individuals and more connected societies. In such a world, the importance of a book on happiness that focuses on practical solutions to modern problems, cannot be overstated. An important realization that I have had from reading the book and interacting with uncle is that while pleasure and pain are inevitable, it is possible to train the mind to reduce the impact of the emotional roller coaster with every pleasure and every pain. It is in reducing this variation that one achieves greater balance and ultimately, a happier state in the long run. The book lays out an action-oriented strategy to reduce the adverse effects of uncontrollable negative events such as the death or disability of a loved one. It lays out the importance of controlling the mind through meditation and silence to dampen the variation of the impact of frequent pains and pleasures. It shows the way of how positive thinking can be practiced transforming one's life continuously to achieve a higher level of happiness. It exposes the myth of tying one's happiness to outcomes but instead suggests investment in the effort and the process rather than the outcomes. The book also implies that while it is not possible to achieve perfection in happiness, it can be a goal that guides you in the right direction in moments of life's choice. Through practical examples from his own life, uncle narrates the choices he has made and how each choice resulted in greater satisfaction and happiness, although it might have caused some short-term pain. The book demonstrates how generosity and giving can lead to greater satisfaction than selfishness. It cautions individuals to limit our natural impulse to expect more and more from others, especially increasing our expectations as they satisfy them better and better. This process, of course, can only result in ultimate disappointment and unhappiness. I hope that this book and the ideas presented therein, can in some measure, alleviate the unhappiness in individuals and make the world a happier place. I hope that it makes people more generous, more loving, more compassionate, and more empathetic. I join my beloved uncle in praying "Lokah Samastah Sukhino Bhavantu" – may everyone in the whole world become happier.

I present this book with immense gratitude and deeply felt humility.   **-- Bin Srinidhi**

PREFACE

Asa to ma sadgamaya
Tamaso ma jyotirgamaya
Mrithyor ma amritam gamaya
Om shanti shanti shanti

Meaning (my interpretation in parenthesis)

I beseech the all-powerful (soul) within me to re-engineer my mind

Lead me from illusion (appearances) unto reality (the truth behind the appearances)
From darkness (ignorance) unto light (knowledge and wisdom)
From death (transience) unto immortality (permanence)
(Lead my mind to) Peace, Peace, Peace.

My family members, relatives, friends, and well-wishers were surprised when I told them that I was thinking of writing a book at this young age (94 years young) but greatly appreciated my enthusiasm in undertaking such a task. Moreover, when they heard that I would be writing a book on HAPPINESS, they were greatly thrilled and strongly encouraged me to do it. After all, they have always seen me happy, outgoing, bursting with vigor, and possessing a cheerful disposition. I thanked all of them profusely. I feel grateful and blessed to be surrounded by such goodwill. Yet, happiness does not come automatically!!

Some people are genetically predisposed towards positive thoughts and their childhood circumstances allow them to develop into people who have a greater proclivity towards happiness. Most people might not be that blessed. A combination of genetic predisposition and childhood might make them risk-averse and anxious, and drawn towards negative thoughts and possibilities more than positivity and opportunities. Some might develop strong emotions such as anger and jealousy. Some might even develop addictions and dependence on substances, people, or other things. The important thing to remember is that all this determines only the starting point of a journey. It is possible to consciously evolve into a happier state over time. It needs some introspection and conscious action – which are well worth it.

In short, it is a journey – a journey where you constantly re-engineer the mind to become receptive to external stimuli and nurture internal thoughts that give happiness and while at the same time, train the mind to reject the thoughts that result in unhappiness. It is a journey in which you continuously re-energize the mind – motivating feelings of love and compassion while overcoming feelings of fear and anxiety. It is a journey that becomes more pleasant as you re-engineer your mind. One also needs to recognize that happiness is not a destination but is the journey itself; not an outcome but the process; not an end but the means.

I offer this book as a case study – my journey of conscious re-engineering of my mind to become a happier person over time. I neither profess academic expertise nor extraordinary in-born abilities. Yet, I feel that my experience will be useful to those who seek happiness and satisfaction in their lives. I intend to avail of this opportunity to introspect and reflect on my whole life, starting from when I was a small child and continuing through my current age of 94 years and running (literally, sometimes!!). I reflect on the events that have shaped me, the opportunities that have inspired me, the obstacles that have challenged and strengthened me, the people who have loved and guided me, the people who have chided and reformed me and the guiding invisible hand that has always lifted me when I was down. I reflect on how I have overcome strong destructive emotions like anger, jealousy, and pettiness while maintaining my poise and composure. I reflect on the transience of pains and pleasures contrasted with the permanence of satisfaction and contentment. Experience has been my greatest teacher and introspection my greatest learning tool. I recognize that everyone has a different journey and experiences are as varied as there are people. Yet, there is sufficient commonality amongst us and so, I offer my experiences thoughts, and ideas for you to choose or not to choose, in the hope that it might help.

Mine is a long journey from the wilderness to bliss. This journey has been one of continuous change over a long time. I initially wondered if it made any sense for someone much younger. If it is a process of re-engineering your mind, does it not have to be your own journey? Can you speed it up based on my experience? My original thought was to write on the subject of how to be happy at 80-90 and beyond. But how many people experience 80 -90 years of life? It is my intention (a rather ambitious one) to help people be happy and healthy at any age. I would like everyone not only to live longer but to live happier. With this idea in mind, I humbly venture onto this important subject matter of being happy at any age, be it 23 or 93.

PART 1

CHAPTER 1

THE FORMATIVE YEARS
- A MEDLEY OF EMOTIONS -

I was born on 27 Feb. 1926. I graduated from high school in 1942. I can recollect most of the things that happened in my earlier years to the present moment. When I was about 7 years or so, I realized that we were extremely poor, and I say this because of a few sad and frightening events that unfolded.

I had heard that my paternal grandfather was a medium-scale building contractor and was moderately successful. Even so, being perennially cash-strapped, he used to take advances from his clients before undertaking their projects. On completion of the work, he would claim and get reimbursed with the full amount. Most of these projects were with public departments of the state. He had a large family with 10 children, 4 of whom were boys, and 6 were daughters. He had a fairly decent house and also had some land where he could grow rice, sugar cane, and other items. The Cauvery River was adjacent to the lands. It also had a huge well to draw water whenever we needed it. Life was relatively smooth.

However, my grandfather suddenly died of a severe heart attack. In those days, insurance was not common and retirement savings were unheard of in the villages of India. His death at once plunged my grandmother and her children to near-destitution and misery. My father was the oldest son aged just 15 years. I came to know later that these circumstances forced him to relinquish his dreams of continuing his education. He needed to look after his mother and the rest of the family at that young age. Remarkably, he was not consumed by regret and remorse. Instead, he accepted the challenge that life had thrown him and strove very hard not only to support but also to keep peace and unity amongst his brothers and sisters. Even though he gave up his own schooling, he made sure that his brothers attended school. Unfortunately, during those times, girls were not given the same consideration for education. Rather, getting them married was the norm of responsibility. It is a testament to his tenacity, determination, and perseverance that not only did he ensure that his brothers continued their schooling but also managed to get all his sisters married without dowry[1]!

After a few years, he too got married. Fortunately for him, his wife (my mother) was a noble and understanding person who sacrificed her material comforts to help my father support his sisters and brothers. Ultimately, my father took up a job as an "attender" in the state education department which was in Coimbatore in Madras State. When the states were reorganized, our town (Kollegal) officially became part of Mysore State.

As an attender with a meager salary of Rs.19 a month, he had to work out-of-town at the District Education office at Coimbatore. Out of Rs.19, he sent us Rs.10 to 12 every month and used only the remaining Rs. 7-9 for his stay, food, and all the other incidentals. The amount we received as hardly an amount that would suffice for a family. I cannot even imagine how we managed our lives with so little money! All the credit for this goes to only my mother. She never complained or grumbled about her fate in life. Instead, she was ever cheerful and exuded happiness. Her cheerfulness made us feel happy and contented. She would constantly remind us of her father's (and her) hope that all of us would come up in life beautifully. She kept reminding us that our present poor condition was just temporary and that we were only being tested by the Almighty, only because we could bear it and overcome the challenge. Her external confidence and inner calm were truly inspiring.

Here was our first lesson in happiness. It is not what you don't have that matters, it is what you have. It is not the material possessions that matter but it is the inner strength and confidence. Complaints and whining do not bring happiness, but cheerfulness and a winning attitude do. Comparing and competing with others do not bring happiness but self-control and self-improvement do.

It is my good fortune that I was exposed to these everlasting truths at a young age, even though we could not eat, dress, or spend like others. Abject poverty is not an easy challenge. We would wander around to collect branches of trees lying on the roadside for use as firewood. I would show myself up at various events like weddings, with an open hand for some cash or food. Cash was generally one penny which was 192th of one rupee then. Sometimes I used to receive a few bananas

---

[1] A system of payment to the bridegroom at the time of marriage. This practice has been made illegal in present-day India.

or pieces of coconut. Yet, however poor we were, my mother insisted that we all go to school at all costs. Just as my father gave up his schooling to ensure the education of his brothers, my mother gave up her ambitions to make all of us go to school. The monthly school fee for us brothers was about Rs.5/-. Our family's total income was what my father managed to send - Rs.10/12!! That is almost 50% of the total amount we got. I had only one pair of shorts and one shirt to wear to go to school. Mother used to wash these and fold it well looking as though it has been ironed. My half pant had so many patches of different colors depending on the left-over pieces of cloth available with our tailor. At least, he realized our plight and would repair it for a small consideration.

Despite all the problems we had, the paramount priority that my parents placed on education is perhaps the single most important factor that helped us all to come out of poverty and lead reasonably good lives. All of us brothers went to the local high school. My elder brother finished his school in 1937 and immediately started working again on a meager salary of Rs.19/- but this was more than adequate to pay for our school fees and simple living. At long last, we could afford to eat some fruit occasionally!! For us, this was such a special treat!! A simple fruit gave us boundless happiness!! None of us ever grumbled or made life difficult for our mother. We understood our condition very well and we started cooperating with Mother.

Happiness does not flow out of riches. Nor does it drain out from poverty. Both my parents had very little to give but gave all to us and others. They never demanded anything; never once did they complain about life. It is the giving that gives happiness, not taking. Ever.

My high school final examination got over by March. In April itself, I took up a menial job in a sericultural department where I had to work amongst female laborers. Their job was to cut off the head portion of caterpillars then they had to pull out the two guts, stretch it and keep it for drying. My job was to measure their thickness on a gauge. Those that passed through this Vernier gauge were made into bundles of 50. This was a dead-end job with no prospects whatsoever. While I continued this job for a few months, my father tried his best to get a clerical job for me but was not successful. Undaunted by a dead-end job and continuous rejection from local entities to give me a simple clerical job, I wrote the public service commission, a written examination. Thousands participated in the examination. Amongst them, several were graduates /postgraduates. The examination was very tough for me. I later received written confirmation that I had failed. When this came, for a moment there was gloom in the house. We did not know what to do or where to go?

But perseverance pays. When I thought over it coolly, I felt that I am destined for something higher than just be a clerk drawing Rs 30 a month. In the meanwhile, my elder brother had gone away to Dehra Dun City some 1800 miles to the north of my village. For me, it looked like he had gone to a different planet!! Yet, I knew that he had a job in the Survey Department. I decided to break out of the confined surroundings in which I operated and wrote to him about my intention to be with him and search for any job. He liked my idea of being with him. He immediately sent me money to pay for the train fare.

In early 1943 I left my place by bus from Kollegal to Maddur and then by train to Bangalore. Here I got into the Madras Mail, I arrived at Madras the next morning. The same afternoon, I got into grand trunk express. I had a 3rd class ticket for my journey. There were steel chairs with no cushion and no fan. It was the peak of summer and the heat was unbearable. My birthplace, Kollegal, always had moderate weather and I had never been exposed to such extreme heat and humidity. This metal compartment had no reservation. It was packed and I got pushed around like a toy with no place even to sit. I was nervous and insecure and did not know how I could survive this journey for the next 24 hours. No one was willing to help me. They were busy themselves trying to settle down. I thought that this was worse than hell! It was a terrible experience. I was crying as I missed all my loved ones - my mother, younger brothers, and sisters.

At times when you are down and losing hope, an inner strength seems to rise and provide succor. I remembered how my mother would say that these situations are temporary and only test and challenge us. Hope and confidence in the future can always show us the proverbial light at the end of the tunnel. After all, I was undertaking this journey to seek better openings. There is no gain without pain!! Even during heat, insensitivity, and chaos, I reflected on the situation and decided that these temporary inconveniences should not deter me from achieving my greater goal of creating better opportunities for myself. With this newfound conviction and confidence, I could even enjoy the journey. On arrival at Delhi, I checked into a hotel room for the night, the room had one dim light and not even a fan. The night was miserable!! The next day evening I got into Doon Express finally arriving at Dehra Doon in the early hours of the morning. My loving brother was waiting at the station. He hugged and kissed me assuring that everything would work out well! I was now totally relieved to finally be in my place with my brother to take care and guide me. I fell asleep and got up after 8 or 10 hours!

Hope, a conviction in what you are doing, and confidence in yourself – these are the bridges that allow you to tide over pain and misery. When situations where you might not have control, confront you, it is not the time to lose confidence. Do not fall over the bridge into the fire below!! Build your mental bridge and cross with confidence. Yes, you can see the fire and even feel the heat - which makes your bridge all the more important.

After a few days, I went out with my brother to search for a job. I had a language problem too. I could not speak a word of Hindi. Kept on enquiring from door to door. Ultimately, I met a nice gentleman; he wanted to know why I am looking for a job instead of studying. He said I looked like a baby! I told him of our miserable financial condition and implored him to help me. Taking pity on me he offered a clerical job with a salary of Rs 30 a month. He also said that he would give me a salary increase of Rs 2 a month if I learn typing. I started working. After working hours, I started typing lessons at a nearby place. Within 4 to 5 weeks I became proficient and was able to type at 45 words per minute! In those days this speed was considered good. My employer was happy and increased salary making it Rs 32 a month! I am ever grateful to him for helping me when I needed help most. I continued working while looking for better openings. Over the next 18 months, I found jobs at different places including in army centers. I also learned to speak and understand a few Hindi words. I was thus trying to improve myself to face interviews in the future if these were to occur.

There is always some kindness in the human heart. When you are down, help seems to come from people and places that you do not expect. These acts of kindness rekindle your hope and motivate you to improve. And when you are in a position to be kind, to be compassionate, and to help another person in need, just do it!! It creates positive feelings and greater happiness for all.

> **NO ACT OF KINDNESS, NO MATTER HOW SMALL, IS EVER WASTED.**
>
> **AESOP**

CHAPTER 2

REACHING FOR THE STARS (AND GETTING IT!!)
- AMBITION, HOPE, AND SUCCESS -

By this time, I had made many friends in the area. From my friends, I got to know that the army was recruiting candidates to be trained as officers in various training schools: I also found out that matriculation[2] was the only minimum qualification required! Coincidentally, the famous Indian Military Academy that trains cadets to become commissioned officers in the Indian Army, was also in Dehra Doon. I often watched the cadets from this academy go out on Wednesdays, Saturdays, and Sundays on bicycles provided by the Academy. They would relax at restaurants, watch movies, and go to dance halls. For me, becoming a cadet at IMA became the ultimate goal.

My brother and I collected two application forms from the academy, and we went over it thoroughly. We carefully filled the application forms and sent them to the sub-area for further processing. After 2 or months, we received intimation asking both of us to report at the service selection board at Jamshedpur, in Bihar state. We were so thrilled! It was indeed an opportunity of a lifetime!! We also felt very happy that we could see the great city of Calcutta with its magnificent Victoria memorial and the famous Howrah Hooghly bridge. Jamshedpur was also called Tatanagar (the city of Tatas) because the Tata family[3] had constructed steel mills in Jamshedpur that extended through most of the city.

On the appointed day we reported at the Selection Board. In all, we were 45 of us who had been called for the interview. As part of the interview process, we faced debates, leadership tasks, and finally, an interview with a Psychologist!! This was very different from taking some tests for a clerical post in the village!! Not only were we completely unprepared for such comprehensive testing, but also it was our first exposure to western culture. It was a westernized place, and we were given one room to be shared between us. The lifestyle of officers there was more British than

---

[2] High school graduation is often called matriculation in India.
[3] A highly reputed business family in India. In fact, Jamshedpur is named after the patriarch of the family, Jamshedji Tata.

Indian at that time. The Mess (Dining hall) had beautiful occidental crockery and cutlery. The food was also very British - soup, boiled vegetables, roast mutton or chicken, with fruits at lunchtime and dessert at dinner, and breakfast served with porridge, eggs, bread butter, jam. Never in our lifetime had we experienced this kind of food or such a spread!! Our daily food at home (if we had any) consisted of rice and spicy sambar served on a stainless-steel thali (plate). We were also strict vegetarians, not exposed to non-vegetarian food, not even eggs. We had to adjust to a very different food that was bland with no spices!! This was for just three days and we both decided to savor the novelty of it and enjoy whatever was served.

The psychologist enquired about me and my background first. Quite unexpectedly, he asked me whether I would marry a famous film actress if she were proposed to me. I thought over it and politely answered that I was here to get selected to become an officer of the Indian Army and could not reasonably answer such a hypothetical question. He just laughed and said nothing further. Perhaps he wanted to judge my reaction. After spending two nights and 3 days, and undergoing an exhausting testing process, we left Jamshedpur. I felt a sense of unease when I saw the other candidates. They were all physically well-built and looked mature and manly, some even had mustaches!! In contrast, I looked like a young boy. I did not even need to shave!! Fat chance I could compete against these fellows!! Yet, having come thus far, I needed to be positive in my thinking. I still had that small glimmer of hope.

After several months, I received an envelope from the selection committee. Opening that letter was perhaps the most anxious moment of my life!! I prepared myself for a rejection letter. I took my time opening the letter. I could not believe my eyes!! I had been selected to report to the Indian military academy on 18 Feb 1946!! I read it a couple of times to make sure that my mind was not playing tricks on me. Unfortunately, this good news came with a bad one. My brother, who had been the bedrock of support for me all these days and played such a great part in my life, did not make it. I was truly humbled that he was so magnanimous and showed absolutely no sign of despair. Instead, he was so excited that he hugged and kissed me. What an amazing Brother!! Such goodness.

Goodness and happiness go together. If you can truly revel in others' success, you can have unbounded happiness!! A brother who feels happy that you got in, even though he did not, provides a great example of how happiness is generated and maintained.

CHAPTER 3

MY LIFE AT THE MILITARY ACADEMY
- OVERCOMING CHALLENGES -

The First Day

As I entered the gates of the Academy, I thought back about my journey from Kollegal to Dehradun. In a different sense, I had embarked on a career journey, a journey of life that had taken me from excruciating poverty to a position that I could not even dream of at that time. It had taken me from the humble surroundings of my ancestral home to the hallowed halls of this nationally renowned Academy. It seemed to have taken flight and had flown right into my dreams!!

Even though I was thrilled and very happy to be admitted, I was very nervous when I finally set foot into the Academy. All the selected candidates started arriving on 18 Feb. 1946. I was one of the 127 candidates who had been selected. Slowly, as I introduced myself, I started to realize that most of them – all of them - were from well-to-do families. A couple of them were from erstwhile princely families. Memory is fresh about the first cousin of the Gaikwad of Baroda. The prince arrived in a massive, imported car accompanied by 2 guards!! Another prince who was selected was the brother of the Maharaja of Patiala. There was a cousin of the chief secretary of Travancore and Cochin. Many others came from renowned public schools[4] such as St Xavier, Loyola and Bishop Cottons, and other institutions of similar ilk. *I was the only one from an unknown village High school with SSLC (Secondary School leaning Certificate).* My nervousness was now compounded by a lack of self-confidence. I started doubting whether they had made a mistake of selecting me or I had made the mistake of applying!! Was this the right place for me? Once more, my introspection saved the day. The selectors must have surely seen officer qualities in me. If anything, the situation was a challenge that I need to rise to. I had the most at stake if I failed here. More than anyone else, I had to put everything in me to overcome the challenge. Mentally, I needed to get over any inferiority complex. I had to prove to myself and the world, that I am in no way inferior to all the others who had been selected.

---

[4] In India, private and very selective schools are known as "public schools". This terminology could have come from the British who distinguish between public schools and grammar schools.

The transformation of thought from one of inferiority to one of determination is a process of re-engineering your mind. After all, the situation did not change. Nothing external changed. I changed internally. I was beginning to understand the power of the mind to seemingly transform situations. Even if the situations do not change, your response to the situations surely can.

As I entered the gates of this great institution I was welcomed by a British Captain. He was soft-spoken and extended a warm welcome. I was allotted a room in Kingsley block. This was like a five-star grand structure. The furniture inside was highly polished. Even the doorknobs were shining. There was a beautiful wardrobe, bedside table, and a bookshelf. I felt strange because I had no clothes barring a few shirts and pants! My wardrobe wore a deserted look!

After checking into my room, we were told to get a haircut at their well-equipped haircutting salon. The barber removed all my hair other than a little on the head similar to a crew cut. After the haircuts, we all looked so different from before, but in a way more like each other. I later realized that this near-uniform look greatly improved the sense of equality amongst us and generated much camaraderie. Each of us was also given a Hind bicycle with a mounted kerosene oil lamp. We were told to keep it shining. Besides, we were given a service rifle that had to be thoroughly cleaned before putting it back in the armory.

The same afternoon we had to assemble at the sports ground for a game of field hockey. I had never played this game before but still had to participate in holding the hockey stick and run around all the time. Not surprisingly, I failed to connect the ball to the bat even once!!

The Second Day

On the next day, we reported at 7 am for the road walk and run. We had to run with only shorts and a bare chest. A British Sergeant led us. Completely unaccustomed to physical exercise, I was very soon out of breath. Yet, I summoned up the will to continue. My physical condition was pretty bad!! I had a bulging tummy that would bounce up and down while running!! At 8 am we had a drill wearing shorts tucked in shirts with an army boot. The boot was so heavy on my feet. It took me almost a month before I could not march in step. The Sergeant often picked on me and would derisively tick me off. We had to call the instructors as 'STAFF' and they, in turn, had to address us "gentleman cadets" as Sir. They sounded very sarcastic when they used the term "Sir". The

Sergeant told us (if yelling could be called that) that when he says "Sir" he meant "Bloody Fool". Taunts, derision, and sarcasm were routine. I learned to tolerate them quietly and without emotion. *Others can taunt you, abuse you, treat you unfairly, and try to mentally hurt you. Yet remember that you have the choice either to accept or reject those taunts and abuses. The discipline to shield yourself from these taunts is the first step towards maintaining sanity. Still better, if you can figure out the positive message in those taunts, and improve yourself using those, you are one up!!*

After the drill, we had to get ready to go for breakfast. The dining hall was as good as a five-star restaurant. The menu normally included porridge, eggs (single fry, double fry, or omelet) with bread butter jam or marmalade. I was still purely vegetarian. Back in the village, I had not even seen eggs!! Initially, I felt revulsion trying to eat anything non-vegetarian. I was eating only the vegetarian part. After breakfast, we were off to fieldcraft - Map reading and weapon training. This was part of our routine every day from Monday through Friday.

Immediately afterwards, we headed back to class for academic sessions. We were taught English, citizenship, mathematics, and military history. Our professors were from renowned British Colleges. They had to do mandatory military service and their posting at the academy was part of that service! I distinctly remember Colonel Gould who was a professor at oxford. Major Washtell taught us on military history. They were superb gentlemen and were very gentle with us. My main problem was that after physical training, drill, and lessons on map reading, etc. I would be completely drained!! After that, a comfortable place to sit made it so difficult to keep me awake. It was very hard to keep the mental alertness needed to grasp the finer points in their lectures!! I remember dozing off for a few minutes a couple of times!

Finally, at 1 pm lunch was served, nicely attired waiters were earmarked to different tables. The one on my table was a very kind person. The menu was all British!! Soup, meat, vegetables, and bread ending with fruit. I had soup only when it was vegetarian, with boiled vegetables and a few slices of bread. I tried this for some time. Slowly but surely, I started feeling weak and undernourished. Even my waiter noticed it and was very kind. He pleaded with me to start eating eggs and a bit of meat. Eventually, I started eating everything to be able to bear the brunt of the rigorous training schedule. I overcame the initial revulsion as well as the guilt feeling that comes from being brought up in a conservative vegetarian culture. I could see others eating meat with nary a feeling of guilt. *Be a Roman when you are in Rome,* as the saying goes. If all others could eat it, why shouldn't I? I "trained" myself to eat whatever was available and not compromise my physical ability to bear the challenges that I faced. After a few days, I brought myself to even relishing it!

After lunch, we were asked to go to our rooms and sleep for a minimum of 20 minutes. The instructor on duty used to walk around to see if we were observing it!! Even our sleeping was regimented!! The afternoon was set aside for sports. The academy was endowed with facilities for horse riding, tennis, hockey, basketball, swimming, and rope climbing. I participated in football (soccer) and hockey even though I was not very proficient. Slowly, I tried rope climbing. My motive was to develop my arms and shoulders so that I would increase my physical stamina and be better equipped for obstacle courses.

The continuing challenges and opportunities in the academy

I was trying my best to improve myself and so were some others. After about 6 weeks, scores of us were ordered to report to the commandant's office. It sounded ominous and all of us were scared. It turned out that we were justified in being anxious about the meeting. The Commandant got all of us together and warned that our performance was poor: that we had to improve ourselves, failing which we would be removed or relegated. It hit me hard. I had the most to lose and I was already putting in the best effort. What else could I do? On reaching my room, I cried. I was haunted by the nightmare of reverting to clerical work!!

The saving grace was that there was no immediate action. The commandant told us that he would give us all one more opportunity to improve our performance. He said that all the cadets including those that were not summoned would be put through a 12-day camp initiative. All the 127 of us were taken in vehicles to a place that was about 60 to 70 miles away. There, we were told that we would be tested for map reading skills and long-distance tactical exercises. I was the first one of those to lead my platoon from base camp to location No1 with the help of a map. Fortunately, I could do this successfully. I felt relieved that at least, I had crossed the first hurdle!!

The long-distance trek on mountain ranges and jungles of the hill would go on for 7 nights. It was awfully hard and challenging. We even had to cook our food in a mess tin during daylight hours to prevent a potential enemy from detecting our location.

I remember that we had to negotiate nearly 150 miles across these deadly forests and hills over 7 to 8 days. All the way, we had to carry a haversack holding our rations and clothing and a rifle. All in all, we had to carry about 30 lbs. We couldn't leave them anywhere and so, there was no let-up!! By the third day, most of us had blisters on our sole of their feet and one of us could not walk, let alone carry the rifle. These rifles weighed roughly 7 lbs. I was lucky because surprisingly I had no blisters!! The long years I had spent barefoot at home had toughened me. I volunteered to carry the rifle of my friend in addition to my own. Perhaps, this gesture of willingness to help a comrade in need would improve my platoon commander's impression of me!! I was determined to do everything in my power to remain at the Academy. When we returned from the camp, the platoon commander complimented me on my performance and for being a good comrade. I was extremely happy that I had overcome the first challenge!! Things started to go well for me. About 10 days after our return, the commander fired about a dozen cadets. Originally, we were just 127 selected from all over India towards the "Indianization" of the Army (that was almost completely British till then). So, nearly 10% of all the selected cadets had now been let go. On the one hand, I was very relieved that I was not one of them. On the other hand, I felt so bad for my friends who were fired. However, my relief was short-lived. After a few months around 45 of us were relegated to the next batch that started arriving. I felt terrible!! I was so angry that I thought the Indianization initiative was merely an eyewash. Such is life.

After a while, I thought about the whole situation. After all, I had not been fired. It was a miracle that I was not thrown out. I did not have to go back to the clerical life that I thought was destined for me earlier. What was so terrible about being set back by one year? I felt better after this introspection. My new perspective was that I had a fresh start in life. My self-confidence returned. This was not merely a consolation. I decided to view this as a God-given opportunity. I became optimistic and started feeling very confident of completing the course and getting a commission as an officer of the post-war independence India. At the beginning of the course a 2nd time, many things I had learned were repeated. I found it easy the second time and this further added to my self-confidence.

There are many events in life that you do not control. Some of them could seem to be averse to you at that time. Particularly, if you have expectations of success and those are not fulfilled, it is easy to give into desolation and depression. The important thing to remember is that your reaction to the events is your choice, even if the events are not. Almost everything that happens in life can be seen positively. Choose to be positive – choose hope over disappointment. This is the only way to happiness. If you cannot control the event, at least control your reaction to the event.

The second batch joined in August 1946 to which we were merged. After a few months, we had the 'King George' the Vth intercompany banner competition. We were split into two companies Y and Z that competed against each other for the coveted Banner. There were some individual competitive events such as Running, obstacle course, boxing, and PT (Physical training). The rest were team competitive events such as basketball, football, hockey, and swimming.

I managed to do well in most of the events, though I had a problem with swimming. However, the co-operative spirit in the team was amazing and I got plenty of support from my teammates in navigating even the deep end of the pool. Another tough event was diving from an 8 feet board. Several times, I fell flat on the water. The impact hurt me so much so that my body was all red!! I was very determined to succeed that even the pain did not deter me one bit!! I finally managed it. Quitting was not an option. My team depended on me and there was no way that I would let them down. It was a must DO situation.

The team-spirit is almost intoxicating!! It draws forth the energy and passion that you never knew you had. You forget the pain and focus so completely on the moment. I realize that it is the connection with others- in this case, the connection with other team members – that allows you to rise beyond yourself in a way that you might never think is possible. Ultimately, it is this connection to others that generates and multiplies happiness. It is important to note that most happiness comes from collective endeavors, not much from individual stardom.

From then on, my life as a cadet moved smoothly. No longer did I feel inferior or unequal to the rest of the trainees. I had also developed a healthy attitude towards work, determination to do well and discipline to work very hard during my non-training hours. On my own, I studied for long hours in the library to improve my academic knowledge for intellectual growth. I practiced long-distance running, obstacle courses, swimming, and physical training to strengthen my arms and legs. I practiced rope climbing to improve my biceps. I set for myself an exercise routine to strengthen my knee and ankles. Overall, this was a period of growth for me both intellectually and physically.

The cadets of the first batch – my earlier batch (excluding us who were relegated to the second course) were slated to finish in the 3rd week of December 1946. The sergeant major (a British) of the academy was responsible to carry out marching discipline for the final day. These cadets – about 60 of them - were subjected to rigorous training. All of us, now in the second batch, were also expected to march behind those being commissioned. The never-smiling and ever-yelling Sergeant Major was a tough taskmaster!! The Academy brass band was to play the marching tunes songs. Finally, the Defense Minister came as the guest-of-honor and took the salute for the passing-out ceremony in December 1946. It turned out to be a nice ceremony. I even enjoyed marching behind my erstwhile fellow-cadets who were commissioned now. The band played lovely tunes for slow and quick marches and finally played "Auld Lang Sine."

The entire training schedule was now focused on our batch. Having spent nearly 6 months as a trainee I felt quite at ease. I began feeling the academy as my own. I had gained much self-confidence and had no fears or anxiety about the remaining twelve months. I never felt any stress or strain. I had finally left the sleepy village I came from!! I was now very comfortable with all the western norms that were drilled into us. These included how to behave in front of ladies and how to conduct oneself with dignity while interacting with regular officers as well as the training instructors. Time passed so fast that I barely noticed it. I was thoroughly enjoying my stay at the academy, including the discipline and hard work it demanded.

Positivity is a state of mind that brings limitless enjoyment. Work no longer seems like "work" and discipline is no longer "imposed" – it is internalized and becomes part of one's habit. Self-confidence also helps in owning up to mistakes and receive critical suggestions with aplomb and eagerness. As you get engaged in a virtuous cycle of self-improvement, you overcome fear and anxiety, overcome negative feelings, exude confidence, and you are engulfed in the comforting surroundings of a positive mental state. This, I believe, is the essence of happiness.

Life at the academy was at times quite amusing!! For example, it was a practice to observe dinner nights once a week. On this day one of the instructors used to attend. We were required to be in our seats in uniform 15 minutes before his arrival. As he arrived, we had to stand up and keep standing till he took his seat. The service also followed the same pattern. We were allowed to eat only after the instructor started eating food. At the end of the dinner, we had to gather in the anteroom for coffee and cigarettes!!

The Independence and Partition

In July 1947, the British government announced that they would grant independence in August. The announcement also mentioned that United India was to be divided into two countries: India and Pakistan based on religion. The date of independence was set on 15th August for India and 14th August for Pakistan. People were given a choice to choose India or Pakistan but had to move to their respective countries by the time of independence.

While the granting of independence was a matter for happiness and joyful celebration, the partition was a matter of grave concern, the time to choose one's country, move there and settle down was just about a month. The assets and liabilities of United India had to be allocated to the two new countries. The boundaries had to be drawn up. The British sent Lord Radcliff to complete the survey and earmarking the boundaries. In retrospect, it is clear that this was done in haste and haphazardly. The British Government approved this decision in a hurry without any thought on how it would affect the people of the region.

Not surprisingly, the announcement was greeted with arson, looting, rape, murder, and loss of lakhs and lakhs of men and women of both these Countries. Millions of the affected people started moving towards the border whichever way they could - by train, bus, bullock carts, and even walking. The emotions were very high, and the danger was in the air. What followed was a catastrophe of unimaginable magnitude. Unbelievable violence was perpetrated by the mobs on both sides on unarmed and vulnerable people including women and children, the elderly, and the disabled. The extent of shooting, raping, and killing was unparalleled and dwarfed even the violence of the war. As neighbors abandoned neighbors and emotions raged, it was as if the whole of humanity had lost its mind in a split second. Marauding mobs went on a rampage. Love was replaced by hate, friendship by enmity, understanding by intolerance, and peace by violence. No wonder the father of the nation, Mahatma Gandhi bemoaned that his heart was partitioned. He even said that this was not the independence that he wanted.

In the academy, the cadets opting for Pakistan were to be evacuated from the Academy on August 13, 1947, by bus to Saharanpur and from there by air to Risalpur (near Peshawar military base in Pakistan). This was a great shock to all of us and we felt miserable, both those of us who chose to stay in India and those who chose to move to Pakistan. Till then, we were all living so happily as a family and now suddenly, this separation was imposed on us. I cannot recount a single cadet who did not have tears in his eyes. With a heavy heart, we wished goodbye to the cadets going off to Pakistan. Even the rifles were divided and distributed. A terrible time indeed! People and countries were divided on religious grounds for political expediency at the cost of millions of lives and an everlasting hatred between two new countries. After the declaration of Independence, we were asked to patrol the villages around the Academy to see if any problems were brewing between Hindus and Muslims. Fortunately, there was complete peace.

By the time of partition, all cadets had been interviewed to determine their assignments to different branches of the army such as infantry armored corps artillery engineers signals Ordnance, EME (electrical and mechanical engineers) ASC (Army service corps) Army Educational Corps. I had indicated my preference for Infantry Artillery and Ordnance. The officer who interviewed me was from Artillery. He was a good boxer, and his first question was whether I was a boxer!! Frankly, I was a little surprised when he asked me about boxing. I was not rattled and calmly told him that I was not cut out to be a boxer. Instead, I steered the conversation about my assignment choices. Infantry and Artillery were part of the fighting arm of the army whereas Ordnance was in the service arm.

Ultimately, I was assigned to Ordnance. Even though it was in the service arm, I was quite happy. My tenure as an Ordnance officer eventually gave me several unique opportunities and experiences. I was ecstatic when I was posted to London to work at the India Supply mission High Commission of India. The four years that I served there were a few of my happiest years. Only the Ordinance wing of the army made possible such a posting. My stay in London is truly memorable because my second son was also born when I was in London! More about this later. Later events show how I got a chance to work with operational divisions and even at Corps Headquarters responsible to look into the logistical side of the Army both during Peace and War. Other opportunities that I got were postings as DQ (deputy quartermaster) in Jammu and Kashmir, as AAQ (Asst Adjutant quartermaster), and as a colonel (Q) of Corps Headquarters, all engaged in front of line operations.

From October onwards rehearsals for the passing out parade started in right earnest. All the British Officers and Staff were replaced with our Indians. The post of Commandant of the Academy which was held by a British Brigadier Barltrop went to Brig Mahadev Singh DSO (Distinguished service order). We got a subedar major in place of sergeant major and other junior staff. Our Indian subedar major was from the famous Rajput Rifles and he was equally very proficient. The Academy brass band consisted of Gurkha soldiers but the officer in charge of the band was from the Army Education Corps which has a separate department for training bandsmen. I was feeling very happy inside over the thought of becoming a regular officer of the Indian army with a bright future ahead. Likewise, my parents, brothers, and sisters were elated. Unfortunately, none from my side could witness the grand spectacle on 21 Dec 1947. The parade went off extremely well. We were then given 14 days break to visit our parents. On the evening of 21st December, I was so high in my spirits. My dream to seek a better future for myself became a reality. I had never experienced such happiness and excitement. Quietly I prayed to God and sought my parents' blessings. My ardent desire to look after all my family members to help them to lead a better life supported by the required educational qualifications to start a new life would happen. Right from my childhood, my only intention was to bring up all my siblings to stand on their own. Never thought of Self. Even now at 94 years of age, I am always engrossed in helping underprivileged families with my limited income. My personal needs have shrunk. I now have some surplus funds for these noble causes.

In the evening on 21st Dec 1947, a red-letter day for me decided to celebrate with few others who had also graduated with me. I bought a tin of cigarettes (50) and beer cans. Between us, we finished the cigarettes and not aware as to how many tins of beer we consumed. I was floating on a different level of happiness.: At the end of it, I went to my elder brother's house to share my happiness with him and my loving sister in law and seek their blessings. But for my Brother, all these developments would never have happened. I spent 2 days with them and went to my parents. My loving Father had by then distributed laddus (sweet dish) to all his close acquaintances. My stay over the next 10 days was memorable. The local people innocent as they were thought that I had become the army chief!!!

I was just a 2nd lieutenant and nothing more. I was invited by many. The festive atmosphere in my little village was palpable. It seemed as though the whole village went wild with happiness. Herein lies the advantage of dwelling in a small place.

CHAPTER 4

LIFE AS AN OFFICER (PART 1)
- THE TRAVAILS AND TURMOIL OF ARMY LIFE -

After this wonderful and satisfying stay, I left for Army Ordnance Corps School at Jabalpur. The commandant was a full colonel. He was a short service commissioned wartime officer. Due to the sudden declaration of Independence and departure of British Officers, huge vacancies arose in every department of the Army. From a Major, he became a Lieutenant Colonel and within a year promoted to the rank of full Colonel with hardly 9 years of commissioned service. it took me 13 years to become a Major, 21 years to Lieutenant Colonel, 26 years to Colonel, and finally 28 years to wear Brigadier rank buttons. Though I was commissioned as a regular officer I could not get an accelerated promotion. Almost all the wartime officers were made regular officers and thus became our seniors!!! Good look for them but stalemate for officers like me. I for one was least bothered. I was happy and grateful for becoming a commissioned officer. If from the tiny village with just high school behind me I could now be what I am. I felt that the future would be bright and successful. Envying others to my mind was a sin. Instead, I should make the best of the opportunity lying ahead of me.

On the first day at the AOC school, we were welcomed by the Senior Instructor, a Lieutenant Colonel. it was not a welcome speech. Right from the beginning, he kept rubbing that our passing out as regular officers meant nothing. His words were repulsive to our ears. He and others have suddenly become regular officers with accelerated promotions. A sense of superiority was visible. Fortunately, we were to stay here just for 15 days.

The next journey was to Infantry School, now in Madhya Pradesh. We were to undergo six weeks of training in the Junior Leadership Course. Overall, we were about 150 all 2nd lieutenants from the second course only. Here the welcome we received was quite in contrast to my previous experience. One Major oversaw this course. As we were ushered to meet with him, called me Mr. Kripalu, and asked how I was? Felt quite at home suddenly!! How he remembered my name was a mystery. We had not been assigned any order to meet him!! Even during the course if any doubt cropped up he would get clarification from Army Headquarters post haste. Was so impressed as a major. but my view of him suddenly changed. On one of his visits to Army Units, I accompanied him as his staff officer. He had by then rose to the rank of General. It was a shock when he did not respond to my wishing him! Guess he might not have heard me or thought of me as nobody.

While on the same course, there was another officer of the rank of Major. He used to take our classes to discuss operational situations on sand models called 'TEWT' – tactical exercise without troops. He was very efficient. At the same time, he was a thorough gentleman with endearing qualities. Not surprisingly, he was loved by everyone. After about 16 years, I was posted to an Infantry Division in Assam. Coincidentally, this very officer now was posted as a Major General - General Officer Commanding!! He was very kind and treated me well. He even visited my house at the separated family accommodation and had dinner. Not only that, but He also sent a nice letter of thanks to my Wife. Such goodness one rarely comes across.

This incident taught me how to conduct oneself always. Humility, as one goes up the ladder, breeds happiness all round.

The next move was to Infantry Weapon Wing at Sagar in Madhya Pradesh. There we learned the use of all available types of weapons such as rifle, pistol, Stem gun, machine gun, medium machine gun, mortars, and grenades we also learned the use of bayonet against the enemy. Overall, this course too was very beneficial. At the end of this part, we were sent back to AOC School Jabalpur to undergo the Young Officers Basic Ordnance Course. The duration was 16 months. With this, we would complete 4 years of training from Feb 1946 to October 1949. This was not the end but the beginning. We were subjected to many more courses. For me, it was a boon. I never had a chance to pursue studies after leaving High School and felt this as a boon.

I had always the urge to be equal or better than my colleagues wherever there was competition. This urge comes to me perhaps because I always felt inferior to others due to the lack of proper education. I always trying to make up what I had lost earlier in life: thus, motivating myself to perform better and better. The 16 months course went off smoothly. I managed to get the highest grade in all the examinations held over this period!!!

My next move was to Central Ammunition Depot at Pulgaon in Madhya Pradesh. It was the biggest Depot not only in India but also the whole of Asia. The perimeter fence measured 16 miles across roughly 800 acres. It was like a gated community. Inside this was any number of huge ammunition sheds, staff quarters, Messes, and Clubs. The Officers" Club became the central place for getting together on evenings, and weekends. We had no other place to meet. Pulgaon was a small town and had no good eating places. Our life was inside our complex only. This brought all of us closer and over time it appeared like a family get together. We started having music sessions, dancing classes, and exchanging jokes. Once every month entertainment programs were conducted. Gave a chance to everyone to display their proficiency in dance, music both Bollywood and classical, Bharatnatyam, Odissi, and Kathak. Those of us who knew ballroom dancing would dance with willing ladies. Over time this became so popular that most showed interest to learn. I was proficient in and very confident about ballroom dancing. Over time there were demands for me to teach many ladies, which I did happily. My boss asked me if I could teach his wife the basic dance steps at his house. I agreed and started the lessons a few times a week. Being in a small place, rumors started linking me with her. I spoke with her husband. He was keen on my continuing, but I was not. I did not want to hurt her reputation in any way.

I politely excused myself. On dance nights I was popular and used to dance with all willing ladies. The Commandant was an Anglo-Indian and he loved dancing. He also encouraged us. Thus, it became very popular. Again, a move order reached me I was to go to AOC school, Jabalpur to attend an 8 month ammunition technical officers course. Here the subjects included ballistics explosive chemistry metallurgy. As I was alien to these I had to put in long hours at the studies, take lessons from a few of my co-students who were science graduates. In the end, I finished the full course with distinction!! I could not believe that performed better than all the graduates.

Soon after completion, I was ordered to move to Ludhiana to command an ammunition platoon. This is what happens during the first to 10 years of Service. This fully makes up what we had missed in our lives. I spent more than 3 years at this posting. Being an independent Command exposes you to manage human skills, accounting, office administration building self-confidence putting one in a happier state of mind. I reverted to AOC School this time, not as a student, but as an Instructor. This was a tough assignment. I had to teach the basics of difficult subjects such as chemistry, ballistics, and metallurgy. I put in a lot of effort to learn as much as I could about these subjects from all available sources and then face the students confidentially. How I managed it is a mystery. At the end of it, I knew that I was very successful. My happiness shot up to the moon!!! This could not have happened without the commitment and hard work!!

During this time, I also got married. It was an arranged marriage. I had earlier intended to marry a girl whom I liked but had reservations about whether that marriage would be successful. My doubts were because although our family background from the financial side was nothing to be ashamed of, it was also nothing to be proud of. Even then, I weighed the pros and cons and decided that it was better to go with my family members' wishes. Once I got to know my wife, I felt more than happy about her cool and calm habits and her educational qualifications. She had done her postgraduate degree in Economics! She was far more educated than I was. Later events prove her goodness in caring and looking after many families for long periods. She had such sterling qualities that I feel it turned out to be the biggest blessing from the Almighty.

While I was at the AOC school doing a teaching job, I set myself a goal to graduate from the Defense Services Staff College. Once you graduate, it is recognized as MSc in Military Science. Annamalai University awards this to all graduating candidates from the Staff College!! After that, I could proudly say that I had a post-graduate education. This generally helps officers to go higher and higher in administrative and Command positions especially for those from fighting arms like Infantry, Artillery. Because of this, I got my first chance to work in an administrative job at an Infantry Division based in the interior of Kashmir. Dividing us from the Pakistanis narrowly. I was responsible to ensure an adequate supply of all items needed including food, gas, and weapons to a force of 14000 men!!

I had spent just about a year when the Chinese invasion of India started in the Eastern Himalayan Sector. The attack was sudden, not anticipated by India and it was severe. Quite recently India and China had concluded the "Panch Sheela" agreement. Everyone thought that we were friends and that after these agreements, we were mutually protected from any attacks!! The attack was an act of betrayal. It was also a wake-up call for the whole country. Nearly sixty years later, now we are much better prepared to face attacks from anywhere.

Without notice, I was ordered to move to this sector to take care of trainloads of ammunition which were arriving one after the other. I had to establish a field ammunition depot to manage the supply. It turned out to be a Herculean task because there was hardly any time to coordinate the troop movements and information was scarce on how much ammunition would be needed at what place. When I moved there, I found that ammunition unloaded from the trains littered all over the place, with little identification and hardly any record of where the different ammunitions were unloaded. Adding to this confusion, there were quick movements of entire battalions and regiments. The troops had no kitchen or other facilities and started cooking food in the open, with all the ammunition scattered in the ground!! As an officer trained in ammunition, I realized how dangerous this was!! This could cause a major explosion!! There was utter confusion – I was in charge and there were none to whom I could complain. It was only by good fortune that there were no explosions. I could only thank my stars.

I got to work immediately trying to clear the ammunition scattered on the ground and organize a system of storage and distribution. I requisitioned labor and vehicles through the civil authorities and started organizing and storing the ammunition in an orderly way at the new site. Simultaneously, we had to dispatch truckloads of proper ammunition to the frontline troops to defend their positions. There was much confusion, and the work was exhausting. Suffice it to say that we were in a precarious state. Fortunately, the Chinese suddenly ceased their operations. At that time, we did not know whether or why they would cease operations but all the same, their cease-fire turned out to be a blessing. I was afraid that because of the lack of coordination and the confusion on our side, the enemy troops could wipe out our entire force had the conflict continued.

After the situation settled, I was ordered to report at the Army Headquarters in Delhi. No reasons were given for the call. I grew anxious that the authorities might not have been satisfied with my role in this operation. I scrambled to get transportation and was lucky to get an airlift in one of America's Globe Master transport planes. It was a huge transport aircraft piloted by an American Airforce Officer. I was the only passenger on this huge plane. The pilot was a very nice gentleman and seated me just behind him. He showed me the beautiful view of the sunset and Mt Everest during our 3 hours flight.

The next day I reported to the officer at the Army headquarters. He told me that I was being considered along with another officer for posting to London, He added that I was a standby!! I was then interviewed by a Joint Secretary in the Central Government. A few days later, I got the news that I was selected and that I should be ready to move to London at short notice. It was a lifetime opportunity for me, and I was extremely happy!!

CHAPTER 5

LIFE ABROAD AS AN INDIAN ARMY OFFICER

After the formalities, I set sail with my wife and son (4 ½ years old at that time), on SS ORSOVA, a fully air-conditioned ship, on 27 July 1963. We traveled first class that was better than any 5 Star Hotel!! Finally, we arrived at Tilbury Docks, London. This was my first international travel, and the experience was truly exhilarating. It was all the sweeter because I never this turn of events. Perhaps it was the reward for the hard work I had put in on the Chinese Front. Or maybe all the prayers – in my mind, I thanked all those who prayed for me. From the sleepy village of Kollegal to the bustling metropolis of London was quite a life journey in just a few years!! Heaven never felt so close!! The slew of good things happening in my life and career convinced me of a divine hand that works miracles!! At once, the turn of things humbled and inspired me. It solidified in me the determination to do better and be better every day.

Extraordinary positive events seem to happen when you have no expectations but still try to always do the best you can. With malice towards none and goodwill towards all, do the very best, never thinking of recognition or reward. Now that I think back on these events in my life, I realize that the happiness that I derived from these events were not really from the events but from within me – the way I perceived the events. If I had the slightest expectation of recognition, that would have diminished the happiness I derived from these events.

I spent nearly over 4 years in London. I found my job as Director of Purchase at the India supply mission of high commission of India very interesting. I was a willing learner and a hard worker. My boss loved my work. On the personal side, my son was admitted to a private school. I lived my dreams!! Everything was going on smoothly. After one year of my stay, we were blessed with another son on June 30th, 1964. My job allowed plenty of social get-togethers between military attaches. I attended most of these, accompanied by my charming wife. My thoughts turned to how I could avail of this opportunity to better myself. I wanted to study utilizing my off-duty hours in the evenings. I applied and got clearance to pursue further studies. It was not clear that I could join a post-graduate program because I only had graduated from the military staff college in India. I approached the admissions officer at the Ealing Technical college which was conveniently located on my way home from the office. I was truly fortunate to be accepted to a three-year post-graduate program in Management Studies there.

    I attended the College for three years in the evenings from Monday through Friday. Ultimately, I finished the course successfully and was awarded the PGDMS (Postgraduate diploma in management studies) in 1967. With this qualification, I was also accepted as an associate member of The British Institute.

I have always sought out ways to better myself. In retrospect, I have been blessed with a determination to improve myself all the time. I believe that it has kept me always happy! Even today, at age 94 plus, I am learning new things every day!! As a matter of fact, because of being house-bound due to Covid-19, I learned to type and typed this book. I have striven to keep myself up to date with technology. How blessed am I to have the opportunity to do this? It is amazing!!

CHAPTER 6

BACK IN INDIA

On returning to Delhi, my priority was to seek admission to the best possible school for my older son who was nine years old. At that time, school admissions, particularly for good schools, was extremely difficult. I finally managed to get him admitted into St Columbus High School in Delhi after a recommendation from The Archbishop of India!! On the professional front, I got promoted to the rank of Lieutenant Colonel. All issues were sorted out and everything was once again moving smoothly. After a year I was posted to head an Ammunition Depot located in Jammu and Kashmir. Although it was an excellent posting, it was disruptive because my son had to be moved out of his school. St. Columbus school was not a boarding school and obviously, my son could not stay in Delhi alone. There were no good schools where I was posted. My mother-in-law and brother-in-law were in Lucknow. Taking all this into consideration, we decided to relocate my son to Lucknow where he got admission into La Martiniere School that had boarding facilities. We felt that although he would be a boarder in the school, there could be some oversight and guidance from his uncle and grandmother in Lucknow.

Barely after 3 months in the new school, my son was distraught. For the first time in his life, he saw he saw a teacher caning a student. He grew very nervous and anxious and wanted to quit school!! My wife went to the school and met the Principal who was also a retired colonel. Fortunately, the principal managed to pacify my son. I also requested my brother in law to keep a watch. To our great surprise, he not only got used to the school but also performed excellently!! Blessings come in many forms!!

My tenure here in the ammunition depot was extremely good. The way I managed the depot impressed all staff and fellow commanding officers including the Corps Commander (Lieutenant General). I was recognized not only for my leadership qualities and my managerial abilities but also for my personality, friendliness, and dedication to work.

In 1971 December West Pakistan launched an attack against the Mukhthi Bahinis of what was then called East Pakistan (now, Bangladesh). Mukti Bahini was fighting for total independence from Pakistan. India decided to support Mukti Bahini and the Indian Army was charged with providing support to them in their fight for independence. Pakistan saw this as an act of war and attacked India on the western front. This meant we had to defend ourselves on both Western and Eastern fronts.

The battle on the Western front fierce. We could witness the dog fight between our and Pakistan's air forces. Early on, the Indian air force established air superiority making it difficult for enemy aircraft to enter our territory. It helped that Pakistan's air force was quite weak and several of the bombs they dropped failed to even detonate. One such bomb fell and detonated just outside my Depot perimeter making a huge crater 7 to 8 feet deep. We were all on full alert and every time the all-clear siren was sounded, we rushed back to the Depot to take stock of any damage. There were regular artillery gun battles that included the use of massive 130 mm Russian guns. We were surprised that the enemy too had these guns, although how and where from they got it is still a mystery. India had an excellent relationship with the Soviet Union, and it was inconceivable that they would play a double game.

We issued these huge shells to the front all the time. Quite a few of the shells were water-logged due to heavy rainfall. All these required major repairs to make them operational. The war was raging in full swing with hardly any time for such repairs. As there was no time to send these back to ordinance factories, I got orders from the Corps Commander to do the needed repairs inside my own Depot as a topmost priority. I briefed the General that the facilities in this field ammunition depot were not meant to carry out these repairs. However, considering the grave situation and the urgent need for these shells, I volunteered to do my best. I could only hope that these shells would function normally when fired. With Corps Commander's support, we managed to repair all shells which were then used successfully. My men and I were very happy and proud that we could do what we had assumed was not possible. The Corps Commander was highly impressed and, on his recommendation, I got a gallantry award - mention in dispatches-. I was also recognized by the government of my home state of Karnataka with a monetary reward. We had worked as a team with dedication, innovativeness, and purpose. We had taken a bold decision to do many things that we were not trained for and for which the facilities were not equipped and ultimately succeeded in doing it. As a result, we had a sense of achievement and exhilaration that was well recognized by our commanding officers.

In addition to undertaking and accomplishing the repairs of our ammunition, we were also tasked with clearing the unexploded shells that were littered all over. Normally, this was a task undertaken by the Army Engineers. The engineers were busy and as I was trained in the use and handling of ammunition, I was asked if I could lead this task. It was an extremely dangerous operation in which we were not trained. Yet, with two of my junior commissioned officers to help me, I set about this dangerous operation. We were careful, diligent, and meticulous. In about two weeks we cleared the entire area and created a safety zone for the troops and tanks to pass.

It was a time of war and our lives were always at risk. We took unprecedented risks in trying to perform tasks in which we were not trained, and our facilities were not equipped. We did not ask for help, we offered it. We did not complain of unfairness but took up the challenges. We did not flinch when danger was staring in our faces. Never did we feel anxious and fearful. Instead, we were happy, proud, and filled with a sense of accomplishment. Happiness does not come from avoiding risk. It does not come from avoiding challenges. It does not come from whining and complaining. It comes from taking the risk. It comes from trying to do things that you thought were beyond you. It comes from overcoming challenges, not from cowering and crumbling at the challenges we face. Yes, sometimes we fail but what is important is that many times we succeed. As I write this, I am reminded of President Kennedy who said: "We choose to go to the moon in this decade and do the other things, not because they are easy, but because they are hard, because that goal will serve to organize and measure the best of our energies and skills, because that challenge is one that we are willing to accept, one we are unwilling to postpone, and one which we intend to win, and the others, too."

The war lasted 3 weeks from the end of December 1971 to mid-January 1972. In March, 1972 I got posted to an infantry division in Assam. I had to move from Kashmir to Assam, from the northern tip of India to the eastern tip!! Culturally and topographically, they couldn't be farther apart. Moreover, the infantry posting in Assam was a non-family station. Fortunately, we were provided with separate family accommodation near the City of Guwahati. In this job, I was responsible for the logistical and administrative support for the entire Division of about 14000 troops. I had hardly completed around 3 months and was just getting used to it when I was asked to carry out reconnaissance to select a suitable area for this division around Tawang in Arunachal

Pradesh. It was a risky job, and the road was still under development. The journey was terrible but was well-compensated by the scenic beauty of the place. With huge mountain ranges fully covered with snow, it was an outstandingly beautiful place!! This posting lasted approximately a year and a half.

In Dec 1973, I was posted back to Jammu and Kashmir - to Srinagar. The good news was that the posting came with my promotion to the rank of a Colonel!! It was a long journey back to Kashmir. Thankfully, I was accompanied by my wife on this journey. When we finally arrived at Srinagar, we were welcomed with sleet and ice-covered, slippery roads. We had to use non-skid chains on the tires of our vehicles. It was bitingly cold unlike Assam, which was humid and warm. However, I had the privilege of serving under a Corps Commander who was very kind to me and my family. He made our stay in this valley most enjoyable. We also availed of the opportunity to visit Gulmarg and Sonamerg where the high-altitude mountain training school was located. I could also visit and pray at the Amarnath Cave.

On the one hand, these frequent changes in posting were physically very strenuous and tested our bodies and our resilience. On the other hand, that is what we expect in the life of a soldier and we bore these challenges cheerfully. In military service, we learn to be happy notwithstanding the circumstances.

I stayed in Srinagar for just 18 months. After my successful tenure of 18 months, I was posted to Army Headquarters with promotion to the rank of a Brigadier, a one-star general!!! Needless to say, I was extremely happy and considered myself extraordinarily lucky to have come from a slum in my native Kollegal Village, rising to be a one-star general!! God was truly kind to me!!

I was posted to the Ordnance Directorate of Army Headquarters. With this rank, I was entitled to display a one-star plate on the front and rear of the car. Yet, my stay at the Army Headquarters was not a happy one. In the Ordnance Directorate, there were very few officers who had graduated from Staff College. My boss and other authorities made it a point to belittle me. From the first day, I got a raw deal. It was so bad that I would be ridiculed in the presence of my subordinates. I had always gotten outstanding reports throughout my career but here, there was no recognition, and the reports were luke-warm at best. It got to a point that I felt it was impossible to continue without getting depressed. I thought about it and finally concluded that I had to quit. I applied for early retirement. My boss called me and advised me against my leaving the army. But I had not come to this decision lightly. I had made up my mind after considerable thought. After all, the last 30 years had been glorious!!

There comes a time in most people's lives where they have to choose a path forward. A path that promises nothing, but material returns is unlikely to give happiness. Choose the path less trodden but where freedom is not lost. Do not sacrifice your precious freedom to get a few more material comforts in life. I had come to such a pass and after some thought, I chose a path where I was free to pursue my passions but there was no guarantee. Happiness hides in strange places!! Find it – prefer it over a pot of gold.

CHAPTER 7

POST-ARMY CAREER

I obtained approval for retirement from the Army effective from May 1978 and became a private civilian. Immediately thereafter, I got an offer for the position of general manager at Kutch salt and allied industries at Kandla, Rajasthan. I was extremely happy to open a new chapter in civilian life and took up my civilian job in 1978 itself. This job gave me a higher salary than I received as a Brigadier including free accommodation, a car, and medical coverage. I started with a strong positive feeling towards the job. Initially, some of the employees resented getting a retired military officer to head them and made some efforts to get rid of me, but I had the support of my chief executive. I realized that the reason that I was hired for the job was that there was considerable indiscipline in the organization and the labor union was unruly. I reorganized the entire set-up and dealt with the unruly union strictly but fairly. In a short time, I was able to rid the organization of the destructive rowdy elements. The atmosphere turned peaceful and I got firmly established in the organization. My efforts and achievements were highly appreciated by the chief executive and I was rewarded with a considerable increase in my compensation. Everything turned in my favor and life was on an even keel. I could peacefully enjoy my civilian life.

Life seems to always spring surprises. Suddenly on 23rd February 1981, I got terrible news. My younger brother of 49 years died suddenly of heart failure that morning. My grief was uncontrollable. I had looked upon him as my son and had shared in his happiness as he finished post-graduate education. Now he was no more. He left behind a young wife and two daughters aged 10 and 15 years. He had no savings at all. I rushed to Dhanbad in Bihar and performed all the rituals at Gaya. I made up my mind to care for my sister-in-law and the two girls as my brother would have. They accompanied me back to Kandla to our house.

I had considerable mental stress after the loss of my most loving brother. My Mother of 81 years was inconsolable. She was shaken and this made matters quite unbearable for me. It was with considerable effort that I overcame the pain and grief and started focusing on the ways and means to settle my sister-in-law and my two young nieces. The older daughter went to study at

Mumbai to stay with her aunt and continue her studies. The younger daughter got admitted to the local school. Fortunately, my sister-in-law got employed as a teacher in the school. In retrospect, I realized that I could not have done all this if I was still in the army. Retiring from the Army turned out to be one of the best decisions of my life.

In October 1981, I fell seriously ill with abdominal problems. I had to be airlifted to Bombay and taken from the airport in an ambulance to Bombay hospital. My chief executive personally received me at the airport and wheeled me into my room at the hospital. I was so overwhelmed with gratitude at this kind gesture and even amid all the agony, profusely thanked him for his love and care. Which officer of his rank would do that! He was beyond kindness. I felt so lucky to have him beside me at this critical moment in my life. He was my savior. He also arranged for one of the best gastro endocrinologists in Bombay to provide treatment to me. He also made sure that the firm's management bore the entire hospital expenses. After three weeks of agony, I finally recovered and was finally discharged from the hospital. I felt so blessed and extremely lucky.

Often, happiness grows multifold during times of crisis. In my pain and agony, I realized the true value of friendship and inter-personal connection I realized the bliss that comes from gratitude. In acknowledging the kindness, love, and beauty of unanticipated, unhesitant help from others, you feel liberated and experience true happiness. I realized that gratitude and happiness are just two sides of the same coin. You cannot have one without the other. Show me a person who appreciates the work of others, is generous in giving credit but never demands it, a truly thankful person and I will show you a truly happy person.

I worked in this organization for over 7 years. I got along with both my junior officers and the top brass of the organization with effortless ease. I could have continued for several more years quite happily. However, over the years, the demand for my finances had considerably eased. My older son finished his undergraduate studies at IITM (Indian Institute of Technology, Madras) and post-graduate studies at IIMC (Indian Institute of Management, Calcutta). I was 59 years old and my thoughts turned to retirement. My idea was to have an active retirement where I would be working at a more leisurely pace while connecting with interesting people. In particular, I was attracted to the idea of settling down at Bangalore City, which was where my wife had grown up and where I had numerous relatives and friends.

Coincidentally, I found an advertisement in the newspaper for the post of secretary to the prestigious Bangalore Club. I was exposed to the activities in clubs and had held various club appointments while in the Army. This position appealed both to me and my wife. I quickly prepared a resume and sent it to the Club. After several interviews over a few months, I was offered the job as secretary of the Bangalore club. This club is a highly prestigious club that was started in 1868, over 150 years back. I was offered free accommodation with a good salary. Although the job was challenging because the club had over four thousand members and my responsibilities included catering to their food orders, arranging banquets, managing the gymnasium, health club, and all sports activities other than cricket, I was very happy because I would be closely connected to a lot of interesting people – the elite of Bangalore City and life would be active but on my terms. Indeed, I was very lucky that this job – the type of job that I was dreaming about - literally fell into my lap!!

I spent over 8 of the most wonderful years of my working life at this magnificent Club. I loved the employees that I worked with and greatly enjoyed the company of the club members who came to the club. Moreover, during my tenure, we had many distinguished visitors with whom I interacted. Even to this day, my erstwhile employees still crowd around me whenever I happen to go there!! Most of the Club members remember me and greet me warmly when I visit the club. After these glorious eight years, I left the club when I was over 67 years old. By then both my sons had settled down. The younger son studied to become a doctor with an MBBS from Delhi University and MD from the premier All India Institute of Medical Sciences, New Delhi. He later moved to the United States and has established himself in the state of Delaware over the last 26 years.

CHAPTER 8

ACTIVE RETIREMENT

Once I left the club, it was time to travel around and see the World. I have been an annual visitor to the U.S. since 1995. My wife and I traveled to several places around the world. In 2004, we visited the famous Lion Safari near Nairobi, Kenya, where my elder son was working. We were spending our time happily traveling and enjoying with my family. I felt truly blessed to have had this amazing time.

In January 2005, my wife complained of severe back pain. The cat-scan showed that back pain was the result of the cancer of the kidneys. She underwent radiation over two months. She was put under the care of a pain management Doctor. This continued for a month and she felt nearly normal. We thought she was cured and felt very happy, but the happiness turned out to be very short-lived. She had to be readmitted to the hospital. Finally, on October 1st, 2005 at 2.10 PM she breathed her last leaving me devastated. I was past 79 years old and felt inconsolably grief-stricken and miserable After completing all the rituals as per her wish I wanted to stay back in Bangalore but my son and others suggested that I needed a change from the environment. I finally agreed and went with my son to Nairobi.

This was a period of deep introspection for me. I thought about my plans. Both my sons love me immensely and urged me to stay with them. I had led a life for 49 and a half years during which my wife took much care of me. Together, we had lived in our apartment happily for a long time After much thought, I decided that the best way for me to be happy and cheerful was to continue to live in my apartment while being strongly connected to my sons and their families. I have stayed there for over 14 years and have been extremely satisfied and ever happy!!

I started thinking about my wife and her nature in the right earnest to draw useful lessons to enable me to be independent and develop a happy disposition towards life. I introspected deeply about my own life. My wife smoothed out my rough edges and brought grace and charm to my life. I reflected on the times that I was impatient and never listened to others. Often, I would be rude and spoil my relationship with others. Like an angel, my wife would make amends and take care of everyone. Without her to protect me, those weaknesses would hurt me.

I realized that I had to change my attitude and rid myself of the negativity in my outlook. In her demise, I realized that a positive attitude in life was the most critical ingredient of happiness.

From my childhood, I had been a very active and restless person. I reflected on this and the one thing that would destroy my happiness would be an idle life. Idleness results in laziness and could lead to dementia and loss of memory. Moreover, I had to reconcile to the fact that my wife is no longer with me. I had to become self-sufficient to be happy. Denial and lack of reconciling with reality lead to depression and loss of happiness. I have observed this with some of my relatives. In one case my relative's wife was run over and killed by a vehicle. He could not bear it and could not reconcile to the sudden loss of his wife. His condition deteriorated fast, resulting in dementia. He could not recognize his children. He was forced to stay in a sheltered place for years until his death. Another relative of mine was a highly educated brilliant scholar. He too went into "self-exile" after the demise of his wife. Over time, he too lost his memory and died an unhappy man.

Self-pity and self-generated unhappiness seem to be quite common after a devastating event like the loss of the spouse. I realized that if I did not act now, I too might go down the same path. I decided to keep myself active and busy all the time during the rest of my life. Positive thinking and staying independently and managing my life would keep me busy and happy. I also decided to make a conscious and continuous attempt to live a calm, cool, collected, and contented life.

Let me mention something about my dearest life partner, Ammani. Before I met her, I had met and had become good friends with another girl. She was charming, pretty, and highly educated. She also came from a highly cultured family. I liked her very much and had thoughts of getting married to her. She liked me as well and her parents too liked me and wanted me to marry her. Yet, I was skeptical about life after marriage. On the one hand, she came from a liberal family that was highly regarded. On the other hand, my parents were very traditional and conservative. She belonged to a different caste and my parents abhorred inter-caste marriages. Moreover, they were dependent on me and I could not forsake them. In my mind, these issues created much conflict and stress. I felt that I had to choose between her and my family. It was a very difficult position to be in and in my heart, I knew that the right thing to do was to give up my idea of marrying her and be the support that my family expected of me.

On a trip back home, my parents broached the subject of my marriage. They had already made arrangements for my marriage with Ammani who was to become my wife. Ours was an arranged marriage. I had a lot of reservations, but the situation was such that it was best to go with the arrangement. Just a few months after our marriage, I came to know from her that she had a cardiac problem with oxygen insufficiency. This came as a terrible shock to me. I accepted the situation – I had no choice. Once married, it became my duty to take great care of her and keep her happy.

She was a highly educated, pleasant person with an accommodative nature. After she joined me, she was quite surprised that as an officer with the rank of Captain with over 7 years of service in the army, I did not have proper clothes other than my military uniform. I did not even own a radio. She came from a well-to-do family and had not faced the penury that I was so used to. I told her about my family's condition and explained how I was the only support they had, to nurture and educate all my siblings. I had to tell her that supporting my family and educating my brothers and sisters had to be my priority. I had sent all my salary to them to pay for housekeeping and school fees. I told her that the thought of keeping even a part of it for myself never crossed my mind.

Looking back, I now wonder what a shock it must have been to her, to have a husband whose priority was to help his own family. Every girl rightfully dreams about her life as a wife. She had to put aside her dreams and share in my vision. It is a testament to her goodness that she never once expressed the slightest remorse about the challenge that life had brought before her. There was no self-pity, no remorse, no trace of resentment. She never objected even once to my ideas but instead, supported them. Likewise. even though she was not a healthy person, she never brought up her illness. She never demanded anything of me. Even though she was young and had to set aside her dreams, she bore all these challenges with a broad smile. She was indeed an extraordinary person, an angel who had floated into my life. She was so good and pampered me with love. To this day, I remember her sacrifice with a sense of immense gratitude. On my part, I did whatever I could. I ensured the supply of all the medicines to take care of her. With her sacrifice, support, and her smile, with her goodness and love, she earned my care, my love, my admiration, and my respect. I feel that what I did was so little in comparison to what she gave me.

She was also a very talented person. In her way, she made our house very nice with simple things. She knitted chair backs and table covers herself. She was also a good painter and she painted beautiful landscapes on canvas and decorated our walls. She cut bed sheets and converted them into beautiful curtains for the doors and windows. It was amazing how she adjusted to my simple ways despite coming from a well-to-do family. She was also a great supporter of education. She strongly supported me in my effort to get my brothers educated. Later, she placed great emphasis on our children's education. When we were in London, she insisted that our older son start education in London in a private school even though it was very expensive and placed a sizeable burden on us.

I feel that her devotion to education has brought much happiness to our family. Our older son got admitted into the prestigious IIT (Indian Institute of Technology) in Madras and after graduating, joined 11M Calcutta (Indian Institute of Management). They say that life turns on a dime!! As a student at IIMC, he met his future wife – a fellow student! Now, they have two sons. The older one studied at Emory University in the USA and did an MBA from INSEAD, Paris, which that year was recognized as the best business school in the World!! He works for a consulting firm based in Singapore. The younger one graduated from Boston University and is presently working for Citibank. My younger son completed his MBBS from UCMS (University College of Medical sciences) of Delhi University and MD from the premier All India Institute of Medical Science. He was selected from among hundreds of candidates. After getting his MD, he relocated to the US where along with his amazing wife, also a doctor, they are well established medical practitioners in Delaware.

My life story is one of continuous evolution – from a poor and hungry child from a small place in the deep south to the father of two outstanding sons and now, the grandfather of four extraordinary children. Both personally and professionally, the transformation over time has been immense. From a time when I lived in abject poverty and humiliation to the time that I see my sons and grandchildren prospering, from a time when I knew nothing beyond the small village where I was raised to a time when I travel around the world, from a highly conservative religious past to a glorious liberal present, it has been an amazing journey.

I have often reflected on whether all this happiness that has come to me over time was purely coincidental or is this something that unknowingly, I had worked for. Certainly, I feel blessed and grateful to the almighty to have guided me towards happiness. I also attribute this to my dogged determination to continuously improve myself and my extended family members against all odds. I have come to firmly believe that a considerable part of success is a combination of vision and determination to move forward. Even at 94 years I am ever focused on doing better on all fronts - physical, mental, and spiritual. I also feel that I was blessed with an extraordinary life partner, my dear wife, who brought grace and charm to my life and continuously sought to make me a better person. Even her demise helped me by giving the confidence to be independent in life and the time to reflect on the important things in life that can give satisfaction and happiness. I want to emphasize that happiness is the result of only small part luck and a large part attitude, discipline, and determination. A positive "can and will do" attitude combined with a strong determination and a discipline to carry out the improvement without quitting – these are the essential ingredients of happiness.

Let me elaborate on what I mean by "independent in life." After my wife's demise, I quickly realized that I could not possibly manage an independent happy life without help from others. I needed help in such mundane things as preparing food. I needed someone to drive me to shops for my groceries and other essentials, to the park for my exercise, to the library for reading and to the concert halls to listen to music, and to the homes of my friends and relatives for keeping my social connections, to name a few. Fortunately, my wife and I had engaged a young woman (Nagu) to help us with washing, cleaning, and other chores. My wife used to cook but had taught her how to cook the cuisine that we were comfortable with. I redesigned her as my house caretaker with considerably increased salary and perks. She was thrilled while I was relieved!! I also prevailed upon her to stay at my place with full access to the kitchen and other places. She was more than happy to do so. It is now almost twenty years since she started working for us. After my wife's passing, she has been with me and has always looked after me most lovingly. Over time, I have come to treat Nagu as my daughter!! I was happy to have her daughter and son educated. It has given me immense pleasure to see that both of them are now well-settled, and happily married with two kids each. I bought Nagu a house with two bedrooms. It is now rented out because Nagu lives in my place. Once again, I feel blessed to have found someone who is not only trustworthy but also loving. Nagu is not at all demanding and is very satisfied. She looks after me with the utmost love and care. I am confident that she will do so till my last breath!!

I also needed the help of a person to help me with other things such as driving the car. With the kind of traffic in Bangalore, it would have been foolhardy for me to drive myself. I was also getting on in years!! Luckily, I was able to find Lokesh, a young healthy man who was 28 years old. He is an excellent safe driver and also a handyman who can do many different jobs at home. I find him to be always cheerful and respectful. He has been with me for over 14 years now. I have started looking upon Lokesh as my son.

With Nagu and Lokesh to help me, I have been able to live independently. I continue to keep a regular and very frequent connection with my children and grandkids through calls, texts, messages, and video chats. I fully understand the impracticality of wanting them to stay with me. Interestingly, I find that living independently greatly increases the quality of my relationships with my sons and grandchildren. Overall, living independently has been a very good decision and has given me much happiness and love.

When Lokesh joined me in late 2005 he was not even in possession of a bicycle. He would come late every morning because buses were crowded and often, he had to wait a long time for a bus. I took to a shop and bought him a new bicycle. I even joked that I would not accept the excuse of a flat tire for late arrival in the future. He too laughed but was punctual thereafter. By the time he completed one year with me, he was very happy. My daughter-in-law suggested that it would be a nice gesture to lend him money to buy a three-wheeler auto-rickshaw. I liked this suggestion and lent him enough money to buy two of them. I lent him money on the condition that this amount would be treated as advance and repaid gradually by a deduction from his salary. This was a good investment in him. He has now 6 auto-rickshaws – quite an entrepreneur!! He has kept one for his personal use and he rents out the remaining 5 on a rental basis of Rs.200/- per auto per day totaling Rs.1000/- a day. Further, about 4 years back, I decided to change my Zen car that had air-conditioning and other extras. The car was in excellent condition and I could have used it for quite a few years. The car had by then done only 29000 miles and looked brand new. The previous day he had brought a person who was willing to pay Rs.80000/- I did not feel the need for this extra money. Instead of selling it, since Lokesh had been driving the car anyway and looking after it, I decided to give it to him as a gift.

He was living in a rented place for the last 8 to 10 years but the owner wanted to lease for a longer period so that he could get money for his daughter's wedding. Lokesh could not locate a suitable rental place nearby because the rents had soared, and it was beyond his capacity. I thought over it and offered to pay a major portion of money for him to lease his rented house. He was deliriously happy that I did that for him. He could now continue to reside at the same place without any rent for three years peacefully. I realized once again that I make my employees happy, they would want to help me with love and gratitude. It is not just a question of compensation -goes much beyond that. As an employer, it was my duty to understand their needs and help them in their hour of need. Getting Lokesh his auto-rikshaws and the house-lease were not just based on cold monetary calculation but an understanding of his need and his aspirations. We must treat our employees with a big heart which draws them closer and create personal bonds which are even stronger than bonds of loyalty. It is now clear to me that both Nagu and Lokesh would not only be with me for the rest of my life but would shower me with love and gratitude.

Let me not understate their contribution to my life. They have made my life so smooth and effortless. Their simple love and affection for me warm my heart. Of course, Nagu's cooking is at the same time healthy and extremely tasty – it is a blessing to have someone like her at home and provide me with all the food I need. She has become very interested in my health and avoids fat and sugar in my food – she packs her meals with lots of love!! Lokesh cleans the house, keeps it tidy, and is ready to drive me to any place I want – as the priority!! I have realized that money has value only if it is used for helping those in need. It makes little sense to use the money for self-aggrandizement or waste it on frivolous whims or spend it to serve one's ego when it can be used to generate so much love, gratitude, and happiness. There were periods in my life when I suffered for lack of money. Now I do not have much need for money - my necessities have drastically decreased with age. I have even stopped eating outside, except when I am with my children or close relatives and friends. Even top elite clubs do not interest me much anymore. What matters to me is to be surrounded by the love and affection of people – Nagu and Lokesh at home, my two sons, daughters-in-law and grandkids, my neighbors who shower me with love, my relatives and friends with whom I have developed strong connections.

It is critical to distinguish between momentary pleasure and enduring happiness. Splurging on self-results in the momentary pleasure that does not even last a few minutes!! On the other hand, giving to others in their hour of need not only gives you sustainable happiness but also gets you ever-lasting gratitude and lots of love. Happiness multiplies by sharing. Use your money and other resources wisely to help others and multiply your and others' happiness, rather than on momentary pleasures.

Although it seems like I am alone, I am not lonely. Although it seems like I have much time at hand with little to do, I am very busy. I pray every morning for everyone's happiness and a greater sense of connectedness, love, and affection among all the people on this planet. My prayer is to my family Deity Lord Venkateshwara. These prayers are part prayers and part invocations. For example, the deity is given many names (thousands), each one of which describes the desired trait. My name "Kripalu" itself is one of the names of the deity and represents kindness. My brother's name "Dayalu" is also another name of the deity that represents compassion. These names of the deity are meant to be not only recited but are meant to call upon one's inner self to bolster these qualities. These invocations of quality set the path for the day and in fact, for all the days of one's life. They guide your mind towards the perfection that you seek within.

Happiness can come not merely from following rituals (they help) but also from introspection and understanding the meaning of the rituals. If possible, you may want to disengage from your thoughts and your inclinations and become their observer. Affirming mastery over your thoughts goes a long way in calming your mind, releasing the tensions, and preparing a way for you to be happy. If you can also engage in the practice of invoking your inner self towards desirable traits such as helpfulness, kindness, compassion, mindfulness, attention to detail, and empathy either through daily prayers or otherwise, it can re-engineer your mind towards greater happiness over time. What is clear to me is that happiness, like much else in life, requires an investment of time and effort. It is a process that you consciously practice, not a switch that can turn on at a moment's notice.

I then go over the book on "Daily Thoughts and Prayer" published by Rama Krishna Mission and read the daily message from the Brahma Kumaris that gives positive reflections. I follow this up by reading a Friendship book by Francis Grey. The thoughts and ideas in these publications and messages make me reflect, introspect, and meditate but most importantly, they put me in a positive mood. Armed with positive thoughts, I go out for my morning walk and a brief workout. Many times, I make time for yoga and different kinds of meditation including Vipassana meditation. Invariably, I listen to classical music. When I find the time, I challenge myself and try to solve difficult Sudoku puzzles. and follow at random. Almost every day, I spend around an hour at the nearby library reading magazines and various newspapers. With all these daily activities, my mornings are packed!! They give no room for idle thoughts and at the same time, make my body and mind fit. My mornings pass off smoothly and happily.

In the afternoon, I watch and practice meditation videos on YouTube using the big TV smart screen. They keep me awake and active. Not sleeping in the afternoon allows me to sleep better at night. A sound sleep at night is priceless!! Once or twice a week, I visit my older son in Bangalore or Mumbai. We go out for walks, watch movies on TV, have a couple of drinks and a variety of food cooked at home. Life and activities when staying out with him are hectic!!

Every year, I go to the U.S. and stay with my younger son for long periods of six or more. My life there is different. Both my son and daughter-in-law as doctors. Every day, they leave home well before 7 am to work in their clinics and return late in the evenings. The whole day I am all by myself at home. However, I keep myself active, helpful, and relevant to their lives. I make my coffee, have oats/cereals for breakfast, bagel with hummus, pepper cheese, hot chilly sauce, and vegetable burger for lunch ending with a cold cup of soya or almond milk. Chetana, my loving daughter-in-law cooks food twice a week on Thursdays and Sundays. It is mostly vegetarian with eggs added at times. The food there is very different from what I am used to in India. Normally, there is no rice rasam or sambar, which are staples in my Bangalore house. The evening food spread usually has lots of salad consisting of greens, tomato, onions with salad sauce, and a few vegetarian dishes This routine is followed throughout my stay. Although it is quite different from my food in India, I find it to be very delicious. Moreover, I enjoy this change very much. I never miss my Indian food while I am there! Occasionally have meals out when our grandkids visit which is a few times during my entire stay. I am very grateful for whatever is given with love!

I make my days in the US also busy. Apart from my prayers, reflections, introspections, and meditations, I keep myself busy with housework. I take care of dishwashing, laundry, sweeping the floor, cleaning bathrooms – and whatever else needs to be done. Although they get outside help twice a month, I am glad to take care of the daily chores and I do it completely voluntarily and smilingly. I also take care of the garden, where I spend an hour or so daily. My wife was a keen gardener and had planted roses, tulips, and a variety of other plants when she visited our son's place. I had also bought two special plants (Lavender Daisy) nearly 12 years ago. All these plants have grown and give bright flowers during the season. I consider it a pleasure to take care of them when I am there.

An essential ingredient of happiness is to keep yourself occupied throughout the day. Doing voluntary work, if you have the opportunity, is great. You could have hobbies such as music or drawing or painting or reading. It gives you immense happiness to be absorbed in these activities. Even doing household chores and gardening can be therapeutic. Purposefully and smilingly, undertaking voluntary activities to fill your day – I recommend it as a basic investment in happiness.

True love, pets, and happiness

My son and daughter-in-law have three lovely dogs - Daisy, Bailey, and Tina. Daisy is 11 years old; Bailey is 9 and Tina is 6. Compared to Daisy and Bailey, Tina is so tiny that one can mistake her to be just a year old. All three are very pretty, playful, and love all of us. Whenever my son comes home, all three of these cute dogs pounce on him and settle down with him on his bed!! He loves them so dearly!! When once Daisy was unwell, you could see tears of sadness on his face. I

am also very fond of dogs. When my wife was alive, we had a German Shepherd, whom we had named "Hero". He was big and looked ferocious but was extremely docile. When he was a small kid, my younger son would put his fingers into Hero's mouth! We had another dog, a pure white poodle, who was small and pretty. I used to take care of their food while my wife cared for all their other needs. Dogs are amazing pets. Their sense of loyalty is legendary. They never forget you and miss you dearly even if you are out for a short while. They always welcome you with great thrill, excitement, and happiness when you come back, with their tails wagging!! Even if you are angry with them for some reason, they never forsake you. They still come to play with you. The true love and affection that they display have an extraordinary calming effect. I have been benefitted a lot from my association with pet dogs. They have helped me rid of my short temper and make me very peaceful. Keeping and looking after dogs could be time-consuming but it is a very pleasurable job. People who have no pets are missing a lot of fun.[5]

The three dogs in my son's place ignore all of us when my son is at home all but the moment he leaves for work, they cling on to us!! When it is time for their snacks or food, they look out for me almost at the same time every day. If I am in my room, then they scratch the door and bark non-stop to remind me!! It amazes me as to how they sense the time!! As soon as I start getting their food ready, they stop barking and quietly wait till it is served. They are like our small kids!! There are days when one of them throws up or even poops on the wooden floor, which requires thorough cleaning. I love these pets and never feel bad cleaning. I live on the first floor. Quite often I come down to the basement to allow these to ease themselves. If you ignore, they will mess up the house making the cleaning job more trying. I need to repeat this process a few times every day. I treat it as a welcome exercise! It also keeps me so busy and the time passes quickly. These tasks may look like chores, but they give me so much happiness. This also brings in a sense of satisfaction while keeping me happy and off idle thoughts.

True unconditional love from anyone, including your pets, gives a lot of satisfaction and happiness. When people love each other unconditionally, they multiply the happiness for all.

---

[5] The illustration is from Wall Street Journal, July 25, 2020 Pepper and Salt.

PART II

CHAPTER 9

TRANSFORMATION
- DEALING WITH CATASTROPHES, AND CRISES -

My brother's death and its impact on my life: The sudden passing of my youngest brother Sampath was an event that had a very significant effect on me. At the time of passing, he was just 49 years old. I loved him dearly, like my own son, and had done everything I could, to support his studies. He was brilliant and lovable but had a worrying nature. I often wonder that if he had realized the importance of yoga to calm his mind, and exercise and regular check-ups to maintain his health, he would have lived a long life. His death was incredibly shocking to me and of course, to my poor 81-year-old mother who was living with me. I could hardly contain my grief at his sudden death and went immediately to Dhanbad in Bihar Province where he had lived. My grief was compounded when I went there and found his wife in a pitiable condition. Her grief was combined with anxiety and fear about the future of my brother's two daughters, then aged 15 and 10 years. My brother had no assets, and hardly any bank balance except for a small insurance amount (Rs.2 lakhs). His wife was not employed either. How could she live by herself and bring up her two daughters? It was a nightmare beyond comprehension.

When she saw me, my sister-in-law broke down and was inconsolable. I immediately offered that I would take care of her and her daughters like my own family. For me, this was the natural thing. I could not even consult my wife at that time. As a practical matter, it was impossible to get even a telephone connection in those days. I thought about it briefly but had the confidence that my wife would back me up in my decision and give them a warm welcome. Upon our arrival, my wife hugged each one of them and assured them that all would be well with the passage of time. I was delighted and overwhelmed by her goodness!! Silently, in my own mind, I gave her a Royal Salute!! It was not an easy decision. After all, they were not coming for a short stay. It was a long commitment to educating and settling her and her two daughters with no financial support. This commitment and support were possible only because both my wife and I thought alike. We were not bogged down by our own limited financial resources and the financial stress that we would have to endure. We were only interested in giving them succor and hope in the short run and help them be independent and make them stand on their own feet in the long run. It takes a heart of gold to make good on such an offer. I often wonder how blessed I was to have such a wonderful wife. I don't know of many others who would have done this!!

It took twelve years before they could be reasonably settled. It was hard on me and my wife because we were also just managing with limited funds. Although I was used to being able to withstand financial stress, it is a testament to my wife that despite never facing financial difficulties before her marriage, she did not even hesitate a little in making the offer. She did not complain even once about a lot of things we could no longer afford. I loved her dearly and felt guilty in making her face these difficulties in life, but she always bore them with a smile. Ultimately, we succeeded in our effort and this gave us both so much satisfaction that is beyond words. This was a challenge that we overcame together – making life better for everyone concerned. We cherish the experience and thank the providence for giving us an opportunity to do good.

Happiness and satisfaction do not come from hoarding your material possessions and guarding them zealously. They come from doing good, from sharing your resources. They come from your willingness to help those in need. Ultimately, your richness is not counted in dollars, it is measured by the love you have given, the compassion you have shown, the connections you have developed, and the succor you have provided to those who need it. The long years of hard effort that you devote to helping others bear the fruit of happiness. In contrast, the years of effort that you devote to hoarding your material resources, often reap the fruits of greed and jealousy that develop into despair and depression. As Mahatma Gandhi said, "contentment is the richest treasure that I own."

Amazingly, when you are motivated to do good, it seems that resources will always be found. I look back upon the twelve years that my sister-in-law and her two daughters stayed with us as the best years of our lives. They provided us with great happiness and utmost joy. Not once did we feel inconvenienced in the least. Looking back, I feel that this time went by too fast!! At the end of it, we were all in much better financial condition too. I was well past 60 years by then. My wife and were able to buy a decent apartment of our own. I have come to look upon my brother's daughters as my own. Both my sons and both my daughters are well-off and leading happy and purposeful lives. My sister-in-law is ever grateful and quite happy. Ultimately, we were all winners!!

The passing of my wife: My dearest life partner Ammanni made the great transition and left me over 14 years ago. I have chosen to stay all by myself in our flat ever since. Even in her demise, she showed me a way to live confidently and happily. I have taken many steps to ensure that I remain happy in the face of many challenges and unfortunate events since then. I will be writing in detail about those steps later in this book.

It is impossible to ensure that unpleasant events do not happen. However, it is possible to ensure that our response to those events sustain our balance and keep us happy.

As I grew older, the news about the deaths of friends and family members became more frequent. It is the way of nature and one should expect that. Yet, when they happen, they can shake you up and if you are not strongly anchored in your beliefs and worldview, can knock you out of balance. I had to face quite a few sudden deaths of my near relatives. My wife's older sister was very close to my wife. Long before my wife's passing, she had remarked that she would not be able to endure her sister's death if it should happen before hers. She was 81 years old and in reasonable health for her age when my wife died. Her sister's death was too hard for her to swallow and she went into a depression from which she never recovered. Just 7 months after my wife's death, on May 1st, 2006, she breathed her last. This was quite hard on me, coming so close after my wife's passing. Ammani's brother and his wife lived quite close to us and we used to visit each other often. Both of them seemed to be reasonably healthy. Just 2 years after Ammani died, her brother's wife had just gone to the kitchen to make coffee for her and her husband and never came out of the kitchen. She died of a massive heart attack while she was in the kitchen. This came as a real shock to me because I was very close to both her and her husband. I was consumed by intense grief and felt miserable for some time. I calmed myself with meditation and prayers. Four years ago, my brother-in-law also passed away. At the same time, my younger sister also passed away quite suddenly. Slowly but surely, I have come to accept deaths around me and move on in life. In those times, there is a natural tendency to retreat to your own "comfort" corner and shutting off contact with others. That is exactly the wrong thing to do. Reconciling and moving on in life is the only sensible option.

Life sometimes knocks you hard. You cannot avoid falls. But you should get up and move. No matter how many knocks you take in life, it is imperative that you get over them. All these unfortunate events so shortly after my wife's death were hard knocks and after every event, I felt terrible. It would have been "easy" to get depressed and lose confidence. But I trained my mind to get up from these knocks of life and move on.

The human mind is capable of wild imagination and conjures up situations that are sometimes very unreal. Particularly when you are stricken by tragedy, the dreams could turn into nightmares. My mind is not an exception to this. I have had several bad dreams at times of grief and tragedy that could haunt you and cause unhappiness. I reflected on this phenomenon where the unconscious mind conjures up dreams that are both unrealistic and could cause fear and anxiety in the conscious mind. This is where the power of affirmations come in. Every day, when I get up, I smile at the world and express my gratitude for another day that is granted to me. I also affirm that all is well and consciously orient my mind towards positive thoughts. I look outside and appreciate nature – sometimes the bright sun that lights up the horizon with an amazing red hue and sometimes the rain that sustains life on earth. And as I look outside, I see small but beautifully manicured lawns, majestic trees, and beautiful flowers. I appreciate the scenery, be it rain or shine, be it green, brown or colorful. You see, the variety itself is lovely to behold. I spend the first few minutes after I get up to cheer myself.

Affirmations can go a long way in lifting the mood of a person. They also make the person realize his or her own power to spread that mood around and uplift his or her surroundings. If a sufficient number of people do it, it uplifts the whole community. I realize that it has been recognized in religion as well.[6] Modern meditation techniques also recommend affirmations at the beginning of each day. This is a process of rewiring - re-engineering the mind daily to orient it towards positivity and happiness.

---

[6] In our homes, we were taught to look at our hand early in the morning and recite "Lakshmi (abundance) resides at the tip of my hands, Saraswathi (knowledge and logic) resides in the middle, and Gowri (strength) resides at the base." [Karagre vasathe Lakshmi, Karamadhye Saraswathi; Karamule sthite Gowri, prabhate kara darshanam"] Only lately I realize the power of this recitation. It is indeed an affirmation of abundance (Lakshmi), knowledge (Saraswathi) and strength (Gowri) within yourself. It is an invocation to these qualities that are within you, to become explicit in your thoughts and actions throughout the day. More specifically, you are exhorting your inner conscience to enrich your own and others' lives, to become more informed and share that knowledge, to become strong and protect the vulnerable. Such a daily affirmation enables you to become a better person who is more engaged in spreading goodness among others and thereby living a purposeful life. I am not an expert on other religions, but I suspect that such affirmations are part of most religions to generate positive thoughts in people as they wake up.

PICTURES

A SOLDIER ALWAYS SHOWS RESPECT TO EVERY CITIZEN

IN A RELAXED MOOD WITH ARMY FRIENDS AND FAMILY

EVERY SOLDIER IS REMEMBERED AT ARMY HEADQUARTERS

EVEN SOLDIERS APPRECIATE SOOTHING MUSIC

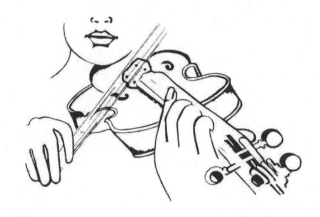

ARMY PARTIES ARE NO FUN WITHOUT LIVE MUSIC

KRIPALUS ON VOYAGE TO LONDON WITH FAMILY

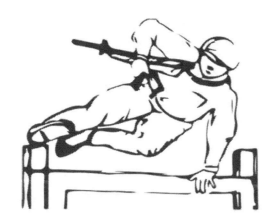

CROSSING ASSAULT LINE ON THE WAR FRONT

UNIVERSITY OF LONDON, MY ALMA MATER

DEDICATION TO DUTY

LONDON STREET WHERE I USED TO WALK

MY PARENTS

RETURNING FROM ENGLAND BY SEA IN 1967

- MY DEAR WIFE AMMANI -
WITH OUR MORRIS OXFORD BROUGHT BACK FROM ENGLAND

HOLIDAY WITH CHETANA, VARSHA, AND MEERA

**- FEEDING THE GIRAFFES -
KENYA FEBRUARY 2005**

**CELEBRATING SAURAV'S UPANAYANAM IN STYLE
AUGUST 2005**

COMPLETING ONE OF THOSE MARATHONS!

CELEBRATING MY 90th WITH MY TROPHY!

PRE-PARTY FOR ANAND & SUKIE'S 25th!

**ALL DRESSED AND READY FOR SAURAV'S GRADUATION
ATLANTA, 2011**

AT SAURAV'S ENGAGEMENT...WITH MY SONS AND DAUGHTERS

**ABHINAV'S GRADUATION
BOSTON, 2015**

WITH MY GRANDSON, ABHINAV, AT HIS FAVORITE PUB!

WITH MY DOCTOR-TO-BE GRAND-DAUGHTER, VARSHA

WITH MY STYLISH AND FASHIONABLE GRAND-DAUGHTER, MEERA

DINNER WITH NIDHI, DEVI, AND FRIENDS...DALLAS, 2019

WITH NICOLE, WHO FONDLY CALLS ME THATHA

**OFF TO CELEBRATE ANAND'S 60th!
MUMBAI, OCTOBER 2018**

WITH MY DAUGHTER ASHU AND SON-IN-LAW RAVI

- WITH MY DAUGHTER GITU AND SON-IN-LAW JAYANTH -
BANGALORE, 2020

**- CELEBRATING ANAND'S 60th -
BALI, OCTOBER 2018**

**VISITING SAURAV AND SHEFALI IN SINGAPORE
CELEBRATING MY 92nd!**

ALL SET FOR THE RCB GAME!

**- MY GO TO PERSON FOR EVERYTHING -
DEAREST FRIEND BADARI, HIS WIFE KALYANI
AND DAUGHTER KRITHIKA**

WITH MY MAN FRIDAY LOKESH

WITH MY COMMITTED CARETAKER, NAGU, FOR OVER 25 YEARS!

**- THE WARMTH OF A HUG -
WITH VARSHA, MEERA, AND TINA!**

**VARSHA'S GRADUATION
ALL SET FOR THE BIG LEAGUE!**

CELEBRATING MY 90TH WITH SHEFALI'S PARENTS, DINESH, AND PADMA AT JODHPUR 2016

MY 93rd AT TAJ WEST END, BANGALORE

OUT HIKING IN BALI, OCTOBER 2018

**- DOWN MEMORY LANE, WHERE WE LIVED IN 1963 -
28 PARK HILL ROAD**

WHAT HAPPINESS WITHOUT A BIT OF INDULGENCE!

SHEER HAPPINESS!

WITH MY ADOPTED SISTER, THE BESTEST - NAOMI

AT KARTHIK'S WEDDING, WITH MY NEPHEW KUMARU AND MANJULA

WITH MY NEPHEW GADDU, LATE BROTHER-IN-LAW, LATE NEPHEW-IN-LAW SEENU, AND NEPHEW GUNDU

WITH MY NIECES, AKKA AND BHARATI

WITH MY NEPHEW KANNI AND SHEELA

MY SAMBANDHIS – RANGANATH AND SWARNA

DOWN THE AGES – WITH MY NEPHEW CHOTU, HIS SON NIMISH, AND THEN HIS SON GAUTAM!

CHAPTER 10

THE DAILY PRACTICES THAT GIVE HAPPINESS

I want to caution that happiness is not automatic. It is a conscious process. For example, I have consciously given up my earlier habit of switching on the television or looking at my smartphone for news or opening the newspapers to get the latest news from around the world. More often than not, crime, violence, and other negative news that spread fear and violence get prominence in the news media while the goodness and kindness of people, the painstaking innovations that have, over time, made such wonderful strides in all fields, and other such good things are not considered newsworthy. Negative news early in the morning could dampen the positive feeling arising from affirmations that sustain my energy for the day. To maintain happiness, it is necessary to consciously overcome negative thoughts and appreciate the beauty and love that surrounds us.[7]

The second most important thing in becoming a happy person is to keep yourself busy all the time that you are awake. A busy schedule fills your life with purpose even as it fills your day with activities. As I am living alone even when I am 94 years old, I find it all the more important to give no room for idle thoughts. I have realized that listening to good meditational, devotional, or classical music makes me calm, cool, and relaxed. It so happens that I love listening to music. I realize that not everyone might love music. In fact, almost no one in my family including my parents or other siblings showed any interest in music. That, however, is not the point. You might have some other hobbies. Some might want to draw or build things in your workshop. Some others might find just reading books on particular subjects (or even generally) is a pleasant diversion. No matter what hobby or pursuit or passion attracts you, doing it – making the time and the environment to do it – is an important conscious effort towards making your life happier.

My love for music started when I was in high school. I had a friend who was interested in and knew the basics of Carnatic classical music. We used to spend most of the evenings together in

---

[7] I am not saying that I did not keep up to date with the news (nor am I recommending that you not keep up to date with the new). Far from it. It no longer was the first activity of my morning. After orienting my mind towards positivity and cheerfulness, one could read the news with a balanced mind. You can filter noise from the real news more easily and balance between the positive (hidden often) news in the middle pages of the newspaper with the negative news often in the headlines.

our local park, where they played music every day. Although the quality of the sound was not good and I could not follow the words, I started enjoying the tunes. My friend used to tell me the names of the ragas. After high school, I almost forgot about music. However, when I joined the IMA, I got a chance to listen to music. Even though most of the cadets sang only western music, I could still connect to it and over a period of time, I started enjoying that music. I often hummed the music and later started singing as well. I have fully utilized this opportunity for many years. The Academy brass band always played lovely marching tunes and I loved it. Once I left the army and reverted to civilian life, my interest in music was rekindled. I spent more time listening to classical Carnatic music. I even engaged a teacher to teach me the basics so that I could enjoy the music even more. I started learning various ragas. Over the last 10 to 15 years my interest has grown exponentially. I enrolled myself in several music societies and started attending most of the local concerts. At times I also attended Hindustani classical concerts. Over a period of time, I started appreciating these too. With the help of many friends who are interested in music, I have collected nearly 500000 classical songs on my devices. Several of my friends share with me live concerts through the Dropbox. They are kind enough to even include the ragas. I listen to these songs in my spare time. In addition, I also listen to music on YouTube that has a huge reservoir of south Indian classical, pop, Hindustani classical, Western Arabic, Sufi, and African songs. I selectively listen to all types of music including Sufi and Arabian songs. I love music with an open mind and find that all types of music could be soothing and relaxing. I can spend hours listening to music and feel relaxed. Thanks to music, I can spend almost an hour on meditation. I feel that meditation "sanitizes" the brain after meditation, I feel heavenly within. Both music and meditation have made me a much happier person. They help me rid my mind of irrelevant and negative thoughts. Not only do they make me happy but also make me feel much younger and energetic.

Even hobbies and pursuits that arouse your passions need to be nurtured and practiced giving you much happiness. I feel that developing a hobby that you like and enjoy, whatever it might be, is well worth the effort and investment of time that you put into growing it. Ultimately, it gives you a purpose in life, a way to keep yourself occupied, and at the same time an enjoyable activity to engage in.

CHAPTER 11

SEEKING HAPPINESS THROUGH GIVING

I am often surprised myself at the change and the transformation in life that I have experienced over time. The most surprising change is that although I was born into a very poor family and literally had to beg for my food, I find most satisfaction and happiness now in giving away what I have. I often recollect my childhood where we had no money even for necessities like food and clothes. As a young 7-8-year-old boy, I would go uninvited to gatherings and festivities, hoping to receive something in cash or kind. I wandered on the streets looking for dried twigs for cooking and heating the water to bathe. Looking back, I realize that in childhood with that kind of challenge, one develops intense emotions. On the one hand, there is anger at the unfairness of it all. In a child's eye, the inequity combined with the inability to do anything about it – the lack of control over the situation – creates a very deep impact. On the other hand, the child could develop a determination to get out of the situation when he or she gets older – a strong will to overcome challenges. The child also could develop a great degree of empathy for the helplessness of others, their struggles, and challenges. The spirit of cooperation with others suffering under similar circumstances is also very strong. I think my childhood molded my personality – at least my personality as a young man. I was very determined to succeed while being very empathetic to others who needed help. Throughout my life, I have never had a moment's hesitation about volunteering to help others in need.

It is only when you suffer in pain, that you come to know what pleasure is. Particularly, your suffering as a child allows you to understand better the true meaning of happiness. The emotions that I felt as a child were very intense. My greatest sadness as a child was to see my poor mother suffering so much and but not being able to help. The only help I could offer was to go out and beg or collect twigs. I never had the time to play and enjoy with other kids. Once I finished high school in 1942, I did some odd jobs and earned a little amount of money. I would hand over my meager earnings almost entirely to my mother. Even afterwards, when I started earning more, I would send all my salary to the family and kept only the bare minimum for myself. When I say "bare minimum", I mean it. I did not buy civilian clothes or indulge even in simple pleasures. I had one elder brother, two younger brothers and three sisters, seven siblings in all. As soon as my elder brother managed to earn a small amount, he would send almost the entire earnings to the family. I followed him in this practice. Even later, when I served as a Captain with seven years of service experience, I continued the same practice and sent all the money to my parents to help educate my brothers and help my sisters. It never occurred to me to spend money on myself. I believe that my early childhood experience of my parents' abject poverty - not being able to afford the bare necessities of life - was seared into my conscience. Helping my parents was far beyond empathy or compassion – it was the mission of my life.

Helping others in need is a lesson that I have learnt from my childhood. My own poverty in earlier years has taught me how much a little help in times of need is worth. Even with the limited retirement income that I have and my limited resources, I give away a significant part of it regularly to charitable institutions and to individuals needing monetary help or physical assistance (service). The "giving" has contributed significantly to my happiness in life. My experience is that by giving I have become richer!! Even financially. Certainly, in my mental satisfaction. I have thought about this. I become richer when I reduce my personal commitments. In other words, I do not need all my possessions. I do not need a large car or a large house to be happy!! In fact, a larger car or house (as also many other possessions) demand more attention, more resources and attract negative emotions (jealousy and even crimes such as theft and robbery) from some others. A less encumbered life – a simpler life – is also a richer life.

The intense emotions of a challenging childhood could enhance or destroy future personality growth and in turn, happiness. The choice is yours to make. In my case, my childhood challenges have allowed me to introspect and change myself into a better individual. The love, compassion, affection, and empathy that I developed as a child have sustained and helped me connect with people at a very personal level. The connections with people – the bonds of love and affection that bind us – provide a very rich source of happiness for me. I have reflected on my childhood and understood the genesis of my anger. Over time, I have overcome my anger, jealousy, and frustrations. I have come to understand and appreciate others, develop positive thoughts about them, and help them overcome their challenges. I have come to understand the power of giving. I help willingly and the more I give, the happier I become.

CHAPTER 12

EXPECTATIONS FROM OTHERS
- INDEPENDENCE & HAPPINESS -

After marriage, with cooperation from my wife, I still sent a sizeable part of my salary to my family. As a couple, we had no savings whatsoever. I felt a little guilty in the beginning at the thought that I am denying my wife the kind of security one expects while getting married. However, I was amazed that she cooperated with me so willingly and with always a smile. She taught me the power of overcoming expectations.

I realize that expectation is often a destroyer of happiness. Expectation and the resulting disappointment from failed expectation is often the cause for misunderstanding and tension even between family members. In my life, I have seen that high expectations from each other have often destroyed the relationships between couples and between parents and children. While some minimal expectation is natural, most people seem to expect too much from others and too little from themselves. It is unrealistic for husbands to expect their wives to be both caring and compliant, never complain but always lend a hand. Similarly, wives sometimes expect too much from their husbands. Parents sometimes expect children to be compliant all their lives to their wishes and also look after them when they are old. Children sometimes expect too much from their parents even when they get old.

Unrealistic expectations from family members, friends, acquaintances, employers, employees, the government, and other institutions – all of them are likely to result in disappointments, anger, heartache, and ultimately destroy happiness. Tone down your expectations. If possible, do not even have expectations. When you give, give with pleasure, give with a smile, and never expect a return favor. Quid pro quo is not a good rule for individual happiness, even if it makes sense in business transactions.

One of the main reasons that I decided to stay by myself independently after my wife's passing is the above realization. While I respect and enjoy the company of my children, staying with them could result in expectations and disappointments. Avoiding these pitfalls has made my life very pleasant. Mutual love and affection with all my friends and family, especially my own children, have increased much because of this decision. On my part, I love and wish everyone happiness from my heart. When we get together, it is purely pleasurable, and we can enjoy each other's company unconditionally.

Over time, I have come to realize the powerful meaning of the saying from the Bible "A man reaps what he sows".[8] As mentioned before, I have helped my caretaker Nagu, and my driver Lokesh, become independent. As I got to know them, I have discovered so many positive qualities in them. Apart from his driving, Lokesh is a gifted handyman and helps me with all odd jobs. Nagu started as a cook but is so caring and loving that he takes care of almost anything I need at home. I have come to love both of them as my own children. They too love me and care for me. They too have come to regard me as their parent. I have heard my friends and family members say that they are lucky to be with me and get all the financial help. To me, it is quite the contrary. I am so lucky that they are with me. In fact, I need them more than they need me. They are young and could find jobs outside - but what can I do without them? Without them, I will have no option but to move in with my children – and as I just explained, neither they nor I will be as happy with that move as we are right now. It is mutual – we are *connected*. My gesture in helping them has resulted in them helping me and overall, all of us are the better for it.

Reflect on what makes for better connections and gives more happiness. In my case, independent living helps me, my children, Nagu, and Lokesh. We are all better off because I reflected on this earlier and made the decision based on what gives more happiness. If I had thought of only financial considerations, or if I thought that only living with my children is socially acceptable and had moved in with them, all of us – me, my children, Nagu and Lokesh, would be worse off today. Make everyone's happiness a part of your decision process. Yes, you reap what you sow. Sow the seeds of happiness and you have a better chance of seeing happiness grow.

---

[8] The saying essentially means that you generally suffer the consequences of your actions. Good deeds result in good prospects and bad deeds result in adverse prospects. Although the saying itself is from the Bible, similar ideas have been explored in other religions. Hinduism preaches the idea of "Karma" – what you do has consequences that affect you.

CHAPTER 13

SEEKING HAPPINESS THROUGH RELATIONSHIPS

Relationship with family and friends constitutes one of the essential ingredients of happiness. Unrealistic expectations from family members and friends diminish the relationship and destroy the happiness such relationship can give to both. Reflect on what is a reasonable and practical expectation, particularly while dealing with close family members and friends. First, the communication needs to be mutual. Do not expect frequent communication from anyone with whom you do not frequently communicate. Second, it is often impractical to expect frequent person-to-person meetings or even very frequent phone calls from anyone, including close family members. After all, younger people have their own commitments with their profession, children, and household affairs. It is important to recognize that as you grow older, your children might still occupy a central place in your mind, but their world is growing and you should not expect to occupy a central place in their world!! In fact, for a healthy relationship, their dependence on you should be minimal. Not recognizing this fact could make your expectations unrealistic and not practical for them to keep up. If possible, you should put yourself in their shoes and see what you would have done under those circumstances. Often, this is not possible because the contexts in which they live and operate could be considerably different from what you imagine them to be. In that case, you can at least try to remember how you related to your parents when they were old, and you were busy with your profession and other aspects of life. The important thing is to reflect on this, understand their position, and create an empathetic relationship where you respect and appreciate their effort without much expectation in return.

I feel blessed because I enjoy excellent relationships with all my children and grandchildren. I love and adore all of them *unconditionally*. We never find faults with each other. I keep myself easily approachable to all of them. I truly partake of their happiness in their achievements and on the rare occasions when they are under stress, I am careful to offer help, without imposing on them. I make it a point to never interfere with their lives. I see my role as a cheerleader and an avid fan!!

Sustaining and growing the relationship with friends is different from doing so with family members. Here again, expectations play an important role in the nature of the relationship.

Unreasonable expectations from them weaken the friendship over time. I make it a point to reach all my friends by calling them occasionally. Amongst my friends, I want to make a special mention of Mrs.Naomi Hass, my 78 years-old neighbor. She is one of the most loving and understanding people that I have the privilege of being associated with. Indeed, she has a heart of gold. She has been my neighbor for over 30 years, and we have many things in common. She lives with her daughter, son-in-law, and grandson. They are an amazing family and all of them are extraordinarily loving and kind. She tells everyone that I am her "best" brother in this world. I also look upon her as my most loving sister. She and her family are always available in case I need any help. I also have several friends here in Bangalore and the USA. Although they are all wonderful when they spend time with me either in person or over the phone, I am ever mindful of their priorities and needs. I limit my socializing with some of them who love to spend time only outdoors in clubs or restaurants *because I like them to enjoy their life their way.* I have had my share of social life in plenty in the past. I make an exception while going out with my children. For the last 6-7 years, I have refrained from eating out often, because of my age. I generally prefer to be at home and eat home-cooked meals. Moreover, I have become selective in my diet and avoid rich food and sweets because they could cause problems. My outdoor activity is usually going out for walks. Apart from eating out, I have also limited attending concerts and movies.

Sustaining and growing the relationships with all those that are near and dear is essential for happy living. I invest time and thought in each relationship. It is not enough that you love someone – it does not assure a happy relationship. The love has to be tempered with empathy, an understanding of their needs, aspirations, priorities, and goals. However much you love them, it is neither good to be dependent on them or expect them to be dependent on you. I also recognize the special bonds that tie us as family members and how important it is not merely to profess love but to manage the relationship so that it does not impose impractical or difficult obligations on them. I am cognizant of the difference in the nature of relationships between family members and friends and customize the way that I interact with them so as to bring out the best in both of us. I can say that this is the single most important investment of thought and time that can bring happiness.

CHAPTER 14

SEEKING HAPPINESS THROUGH A SPIRITUAL QUEST

Before my wife's passing 14 years ago, the idea of getting involved in a spiritual quest had never occurred to me. My wife's death was a traumatic event for me. She suffered from kidney cancer that spread all over, resulting in great pain and agony, and finally her death. She was so dear to me that this process of cancer's painful progression became unbearable for me. I suffered in silence and loneliness even before she died. When she left and I felt all alone in life at the age of 80, I became restless and was in the dark as to how to continue with my life. I did not want my grief and shock to lead me to depression. I needed to regain my confidence and make an effort to live by myself happily, not miserably. I suddenly realized the need to get over my unbearable grief first, and then find peace and happiness. I tried to read about it and discussed it with some well-meaning acquaintances. I desperately wanted to overcome the shock to lead a happy and contented life. That was the first time in my life that I seriously thought of seeking spiritual solace to console my mind and heal my heart.

Fortunately, a branch of Ramakrishna Mission was located nearby. I visited the place and found an atmosphere of serenity, quiet peace, and silence. I approached one of the Swamijis[9] and sought his help. He was kind and helpful. He suggested that I start every morning reading holy books. He recommended one of their publications – a book that was written 100 years back by swami Paramanandaji titled "Daily Thoughts and Prayers". This book was available in their own library. The Swamiji also recommended daily meditation in their spacious hall. I dutifully followed his advice and started both reading the book in the morning and meditating in their hall. This change in my lifestyle made me feel better and more inward-looking. I started meditating on the teachings of Sri Ramakrishna Paramahamsa daily at the Ashram. I became deeply engaged in the practice of meditation, so much so that I even started dreaming about it even while sleeping. I could feel a dramatic change in me. I felt calm and peaceful by concentrating on meditation and recollecting the golden words of advice so beautifully explained in that Holy Book.

---

[9] Spiritual counselors

I had the habit of switching on the TV for news and simultaneously glancing at the daily newspapers in the mornings. These papers generally highlight negative events such as murders, rapes, and other similar unhappy incidents because they attract the attention of more people and in turn, would increase the revenue of the newspaper. However, reading such negative news disturbs the mind early in the morning. It produces negative thoughts, anger, frustration, and disappointment. It sets the tone for the whole day and in turn, destroys peace and happiness. I decided to give up this habit and substitute it with reading the book of daily thoughts and prayers first thing in the morning. This creates positive thoughts that set the tone for the day. I started following it up by offering prayers by reciting their Holy Book daily. in the mornings. I also sought out spiritual programs like Bhajans, meditation-videos, and religious music. spiritual programs on TV and radio. For fourteen years, I have practiced this routine every day. It has become habitual and at the same time, has given me peace and happiness in life as well as the energy and confidence to lead a meaningful and purposeful life.

Another outcome of my spiritual journey is that of continuous self-improvement. I am always on the lookout for materials to improve my spiritual thinking to become peaceful and happy. In order to keep physically fit, I turned to yoga. I had done a yoga course over 40 years ago. The course was offered by the Divine Life Society headquartered at Rishikesh, Hardwar. This short 10-day course was conducted at Adipur, Kutch, where I was staying at that time. I remember that the course was of a one-hour duration every day. My Guru for this yoga Course was of German Origin. He was handsome and had a glow on his face that comes from a near-perfect physique. When I was in the army service, we maintained our physical fitness by fast exercises such as running, physical training, boxing, playing hockey, football, basketball, tennis, and squash. We were taught horse-riding too. Unlike those physically exhausting exercises, yoga focuses on a comprehensive and coordinated body and mind control. It emphasizes the achievement of balance rather than building muscles and developing bodily strength. It emphasizes body flexibility and coordinated breathing rather than working out to exhaust the body. Even then, I recalled that I found yoga to be tough, but managed to complete the course. As we grow older, controlled movements of yoga have a less adverse effect on the body compared to the jerky and fast movements of modern exercises that could result in injuries and have adverse side-effects.

CHAPTER 15

MEDITATION AND HAPPINESS

About 13 years ago I was traveling to Hongkong via Bangkok (Thailand) from Bombay. On the plane, sitting next to me was a friendly Australian lady and we had a long conversation. During the course of the conversation, she mentioned that she had gone to Bombay to undergo a course on Vipassana. She explained to me that this meditation was of Buddhist origin. She had practiced vipassana for quite a few years. When she talked about it, I felt embarrassed that I had never heard of it, even though I was a local Indian where the practice of vipassana originated and where it is flourishing. It was awkward but I must admit that most Indians are more familiar with western methods and even recognitions compared to their own heritage. Vipassana is a Buddhist form of the Sanskrit word "Vipashyana", which literally means 'special seeing' or 'intense or powerful seeing' [the concept is to observe oneself intensely from outside – you become both the subject and object of observation). I stayed for three weeks in Hongkong with a close relative. The atmosphere in their house was very peaceful and it was like being in a retreat!!

On my return to Bangalore, I checked for a Vipassana center and found one in Bangalore itself. I reached out to them and found a slot on a fresh ten-day course that was to start in two weeks. Even food and accommodation were free!! I was told that no pre-study was required for the course. As advised, I reported at 2 PM on the first day at the location that was about 30 miles away on Bangalore-Tumkur Road. There were about 25 of us and we were welcomed and were asked to deposit all items like cell phone, money, books, etc. For each one of us, they wrapped and sealed our items, and deposited them in their locker. We were not allowed to use any of these during the entire course.

At 5:30 PM, we gathered in their meditation hall for a briefing. One of the instructors extended a warm welcome and told us clearly that the purpose, of course, was to help us improve our concentration. We were told to observe total silence for all the ten days. The only time we could talk was to answer anything that the instructor asked. We were told to report the next morning at 4:30 AM sharp at the Buddha Meditation Hall. We had to get up fairly early to be able to arrive at the appointed time. No tea or coffee was served before the appointment. During the first three days, we were told to just observe our breathing in and out and nothing else. Surprisingly, after a day or two, we were able to concentrate a lot better for a lot longer than when we started. The first session finished after an hour and a half at 6 AM. We were then served a hot and delicious breakfast with tea/coffee. We reported back at the meditation hall at 8 AM to continue our observation of breathing for three more hours till 11 AM. Lunch was served from 11 AM to 12 noon. Thereafter, we had a one-hour question-answer session with our Instructor. Then we were allowed to rest up to 3 PM and had another meditation session for 2 hours till 5 PM. Dinner was served at 6 PM and we were back for the final session of the day lasting about one hour.

The meditation sessions were jam-packed. This regimen of meditating in total silence for 7 to 8 hours a day is very tough, particularly for active people who are used to a lot of conversation and activity. After about 3 or 4 days, several participants could not manage and left. Although I was the oldest person in my batch, I was very determined to complete the course, with a spirit and a will to learn. I managed to complete the entire ten-day course. I should admit that it seemed like ten months!!! It is only a strong will and the power of the mind that allowed me to sustain the regimen and complete the course. I realized that immense mental determination is vital to bear the stress of long hours of sitting and concentrating. For me, the most difficult part was to keep silent all the time!! I am used to talking and chatting most of the time and I had to use all my willpower to complete the course.

On the last day of the course, all of us and our instructors assembled, and we were asked to give our views on the usefulness of the Course. I praised the instructors for their devotion and commitment and thanked them for serving delicious food for 10 days! I applauded them profusely for imparting valuable lessons that could help me in becoming a happy person. I mentioned that although observing silence was difficult for me, I had improved my concentration through the long hours of meditation. Before leaving, I made a small donation to help the organization.

To this day, I continue to meditate twice a day. It has become a habit now, and I find that it has the effect of cleansing the mind. This course has motivated me to delve deeper into myself to realize the divinity inside me. Over time, meditation, concentration, and introspection have reoriented my personality and made me a different person. This practice has cleared my thought process and I have a feeling that I now have a new lease of life. I have become more engaged in what goes on around me without getting entangled in it. I have become more mindful of the things that I do and the consequences my actions have on me and others. I have also started reading more on the subject of meditation. Besides, I watch meditation videos from various countries on YouTube.

I am still very attached to the Ramakrishna Mission. After all, this was the place that started me on my spiritual journey after my wife's passing away. Whenever I am in Bangalore, I visit their center regularly to meditate in their vast and beautiful prayer hall. The silence, peace, and serenity of the place make it a perfect place for meditative practices. A beautiful and majestic marble statue of Ramakrishna Paramahamsa on a pedestal in the hall inspires me. The very look of this sage, so simply attired and yet so wise, bestows on me a heavenly bliss. To me, he is an incarnation of God!! The adjacent room has a statue of the venerable Sharada Devi, a symbol of purity, divinity, and simplicity. When I am in the center, I feel as if I am in the presence of these divine incarnations. I often feel an outburst of love and respect for them, and for the whole of humanity. These feelings have only intensified over time. I feel so blessed to have this center so accessible to me. I have also taken part in several of their meditation programs and have benefitted immensely from them.

After my exposure to meditation and spirituality both in the Ramakrishna Mission and during the Vipassana course, my ability to be happy and peaceful has grown exponentially. It has also inspired me to look out for more opportunities to better myself. Around the corner of my apartment, there is a three-storied Brahmakumari Center. I had never visited this center. I visited them and realized that it is an international organization that has centers all over the globe. It is run entirely by women referred to as Brahmakumaris. Their headquarters is at Mount Abu. The center was established in 1930 at Hyderabad, Sindh, now part of Pakistan. They teach Raja Yoga that combines meditation practice with spiritual self-knowledge. Here is a description of Raja Yoga from their website:

"Raja Yoga meditation is a form of meditation that is accessible to people of all backgrounds. It is a meditation without rituals or mantras and can be practiced anywhere at any time. Raja Yoga meditation is practiced with 'open eyes', which makes this method of meditation versatile, simple, and easy to practice. Meditation is a state of being in that place just beyond everyday consciousness, which is where spiritual empowerment begins. Spiritual awareness gives us the power to choose good and positive thoughts over those, which are negative and wasteful. We start to respond to situations, rather than just reacting to them. We begin to live with harmony, we create better and happier,

healthier relationships and change our lives in a most positive way."

(https://www.brahmakumaris.org/meditation/raja-yoga-meditation)

When I visited the center, the guide welcomed me warmly and took me to all three floors. The entire place is managed by Brahma Kumaris clad in sparkling white sarees. I came to know they run a seven-day orientation course on Raja Yoga. One of the Brahma Kumaris introduced herself and asked whether I was ready to take the orientation course. I was intrigued and said yes – and thus began my orientation course. In addition, I started attending the Center to meditate and listen to their daily sermons called "Murali" in the evenings. I was highly impressed and began alternating meditating at Rama Krishna Mission and Brahma Kumari Center. I also enrolled to receive their positive reflection messages which I receive daily every morning except Sundays. These are very good positive thoughts and put me in a positive mood the first thing in the morning. I feel the difference. I feel charged and energized with these positive thoughts every day.

There are some differences between these different schools of meditation practice. For example, in Vipassana, you concentrate on breathing. With Brahma Kumaris' meditation practice, you concentrate on the center of the forehead between the eyes. In both cases, the focus and concentration develop as you practice more. The inner feeling of satisfaction that one gets is experiential and is difficult to describe in words. As I got deeper into the Brahma Kumari practice, I experienced the spot becoming brighter and I got the feeling of being elevated and getting closer to my own inner conscience. Both these practices have had transformational effects on me. At the end of each meditation session, I get a heavenly feeling – a feeling of bliss and joy.

I am struck by the fact that although different meditation practices have evolved in different cultures, all of them have one common thread – they are meant to calm your mind, make you more mindful, increase your concentration, increase the positivity of your thoughts, and disengage you from getting too involved in the negative cycle of thoughts and actions. These practices have enabled me to view my thoughts as an observer rather than follow them like a slave. They have allowed me to control my thoughts rather than my thoughts controlling me. In a way, they have liberated me from my own thoughts.

CHAPTER 16

THE WISDOM IN SAYINGS AND QUOTATIONS

Apart from practicing meditation, I also started reading articles and books on meditation. While I will not go into summarizing all the insights embedded in those works, I will give some quotations that seem to summarize the wisdom of all the works.

Here are some quotes from Swami Sivananda Saraswati:

"Decreasing happiness in the midst of increasing comforts…" This addresses the question of why we acquire possessions and how we get so attached to them that they control our thoughts rather than us controlling their use. Mahatma Gandhi was a great proponent of dispossession. The more you dispossess, i.e., give away your possessions, the happier you become. In fact, the Mahatma literally gave up all his worldly possessions and lived on the goodness and kindness of others. Although it might not be practical for most of us to achieve that level of dispossession, the essence of the teaching is to disengage from material possessions so that your mind is not enslaved by them."

"We may often give without love, but we can never love without giving." I have come to slowly realize the power of this saying. Much of philanthropy and charity are incentivized by mundane considerations such as tax advantages and prevailing norms. Giving without love is quite common. It is good but it does not provide much happiness for the donor. On the other hand, the idea of love is to treat the other person as part of yourself. It is unconditional. I note that while compassion is conditional (I give because the other person is suffering and needs help), affection is unconditional (I give because I like the person – irrespective of whether that person needs or does not need help), But love transcends affection in that it treats the other person as part of you. In that sense, you are not really giving to someone else – that thought does not even arise. This is the concept of universal love – exemplified by say, a mother's love for her baby.

"Be Good, Do Good…." It is a variant of the preceding saying. One needs to purify oneself and become good that facilitates doing good to others – positive in thoughts, encouraging and inspirational in words, and helpful in actions.

Here are some other quotations that convey much insight:

"Happiness is when you think, what you say and what you do are in harmony..." Reflecting on this quotation, I realize that achieving happiness is not a one-dimensional endeavor. It requires harmonization across my thoughts, words, and actions. The process of re-engineering towards a happier state of being is, therefore, a process of re-engineering not merely the thoughts but also how I communicate with others (words) and the actions I take to implement those thoughts and words (actions). Many scholars have written about happiness, but I cannot become happy just by reading and "understanding" what they say. It is good to read them and transform my thoughts to become more positive, loving, and helpful but it is also important that in my daily life I say loving words, encourage positive thoughts in others and truly help others to overcome their own struggles in life.

"For every minute you are angry you lose sixty seconds of happiness." In a very practical sense, anger is the poison that destroys happiness. I recognize that there are two types of anger. The first is reactive anger – where one loses temper and exhibits a fit of rage in reaction to a situation. This type of anger is a short-term aberration for the person but could result in a lifelong loss of a relationship or connection. It is essential to control this emotion and overcome it completely to have any hope of becoming happy in life. The second kind of anger is proactive anger. It is the burning anger within you that results in your spending a lot of time planning revenge against someone who might have wronged you. Sometimes, anger about a social system that does not work could make you come up with an alternative and better system. However, in most cases, proactive anger is sinister and harmful to both the one who is angry and the one at whom the anger is directed. Most of terrorism in the world, the wars that are fought, are examples of proactive anger. Overcoming proactive anger requires even more effort than overcoming reactive anger. A continuous negation of negative thoughts, even against those that you think have wronged and harmed you and replacing them with at least neutral if not positive thoughts, is the only way that proactive anger can be overcome. The point of all these quotes is that they have helped me in reflecting, introspecting, and thereby improving my own thoughts, words, and actions. I suggest that the readers who seek happier lives could look up a few of these quotations, available in the thousands. Almost all of them can trigger a process of reflection and introspection. Ultimately, it is the reflection and introspection that help in the process of transformation.

CHAPTER 17

PRACTICAL MATTERS AND TRAITS THAT LEAD TO HAPPINESS

a. Independence, Active living, and Happiness

Independent living: I began to understand the value of staying all by myself after my wife's demise. Although both my sons were welcoming of me into their homes, living independently was one of the most important decisions that have given me happiness. First, it has given me self-confidence that I can manage my affairs – all my affairs - independently. It has given me the liberty to do what I want and the way I want. I make mistakes but I am not judged on those mistakes. I can learn from my mistakes and move forward ever more confidently. I do my own shopping and attend to both the small and the big problems that come with the house, the car, or the people. For example, say there is internet disruption or the invertor (back-up power generator) stops functioning, or the washing machine or refrigerator stops functioning or the TV loses the cable link. To set these matters right, I need to apply my mind, identify the right person to handle the task on hand, and make decisions on choosing the best person for the job. I quickly recognized that it is not trivial to keep the house running smoothly. It demands much attention in arriving at the plan of action and then, the related activities keep me busy. While I looked upon these problems as annoying and the chores as routine earlier, I have come to realize their value. Now, I do not consider them annoyances but love managing the house. I happily accept all these tasks and responsibilities that keep me busy from the morning to the night.

While it is important to be busy with daily household activities and the like, I would also mention that developing an overall purpose at every stage is important. Physical, intellectual, and spiritual activities go hand-in-hand and to the extent that they are oriented towards one or more purposes, they yield even more happiness and satisfaction. As a case in point, in 2017, at the age of 91, my drive to continue challenging myself to run in marathons propelled me to complete my 8th marathon. I felt immense satisfaction that I had completed it without any problem. I was energized to write my first book – an autobiography with the title "Marathon at 90" In July of that year. Challenging myself with both physical activity and intellectual pursuits provides me with a purpose, fills me with energy, and results in boundless gratification and happiness. The book received several good reviews and generated good sales. I am gratified that after three years, there is still a lot of demand from new readers. As I write this book on happiness, at age 94, I feel the same surge of energy and purpose that I felt earlier. If all goes well, I should be able to launch this book by the end of this year.

There are three aspects to the activities that are essential to being happy. First, I cannot emphasize enough the importance of keeping myself busy. An idle mind is indeed the devil's workshop and the main product of that workshop is unhappiness!! Challenging oneself to higher levels of physical activities and intellectual pursuits result in tangible purposes in life and incrementally yield much greater satisfaction and happiness. Second, I try every day to balance different kinds of activities – physical activities, mental activities, meditation, entertainment, and connecting with people. The third aspect is one of regularity and routine. Regularity is the allocation of time to different activities during the day. Routine is doing the same activities every day. Regularity is essential for happiness. The routineness could differ among individuals, but routine brings comfort. Regularity and routine give purpose to everyday living!! Together, they nurture happiness and allow it to blossom.

b. Smiling -The Essence of Happiness

Often, it is said that happy people smile because they have something to smile about. I feel that it is like putting the cart before the horse. Smiling can make one happy!! This is something that is not well recognized. It is said that smiling makes one look younger, that it takes sixty muscles to frown but only thirteen to smile. Another common statement is that the shortest distance between two people is a smile. Smiling creates a positive and confident feeling of wellbeing. It creates an atmosphere that is conducive to the growth of happiness and pleasantness. It breaks the ice, lightens the environment, encourages openness and camaraderie, encourages humor, and strengthens the connections with all people around you. Whenever I meet anyone, I welcome them with a broad smile and at once the atmosphere seems bright and immediately creates a feeling of closeness. On the contrary, I have seen that a long face quickly alienates all those around you.

Once I realized this about a decade back, the power of a smile in making me and all the others around me happy, I have been assiduously practicing it daily in my life. A smile is also the outward expression of the positive feeling inside. When I meet someone and they talk about something nice that happened to them or their family, I make it a point to engage in their happiness and not only display excitement but feel that excitement. When they talk about something troubling, I try to empathize with them and see how I can help them bring that smile back!! Amazingly, practicing this has changed my own nature. Such is the power of a smile. Every smile you give comes back with many a smile in return.

Smiling is essential to improving happiness in one's life. When I get up every morning, I start with a positive thought and say to myself that I am happy, healthy, free, and abundant. I say it till I feel it and then I smile at the world around me. As I have mentioned elsewhere, I have consciously practiced feeling good in the morning – being grateful for a new day (in my life), appreciative of the beauty of nature, be it snowy, rainy or shiny!! I find plenty of things to smile about every morning.

Humor in life can also lighten the atmosphere and bring a smile to one's face. I am greatly appreciative of humor even though I am not good at remembering jokes and coming up with humor-filled conversations in a gathering. All the same, I enjoy the humor and make myself happier.

After I transformed myself to have positive thoughts and smiles every day, I found to my surprise that it also has many health benefits. For example, it has helped in regulating my BP (Blood Pressure), increased my sleep, and improved my digestion. It has motivated me to remain physically and mentally very active. It has brought a sense of continuous joy and contentment. I feel very blessed and grateful to be in such a good shape with hardly any medical issues.
Once again, let us all smile!! It costs nothing but is worth millions. Keep smiling always!!

c. Grit, Determination, And Perseverance

I have realized that it is important to continuously challenge both the body and the mind to keep fit, a precondition for happiness. It is also true that as one gets older, certain physical abilities and the reflex action deteriorates. Therefore, the physical challenges one looks for at an older age are likely different from the physical challenges one looks for at a younger age. It is a matter of balance to choose a proper challenge – one that is not easy but one that can be achieved. *The important thing is to never stop looking for challenges.*

I am always looking for challenges to motivate and keep me going forward. One such challenge that I took upon myself was to learn backstroke in swimming when I was then 89 years old. I had learnt to swim during my training at the Military Academy. I had become quite proficient in freestyle swimming. However, I had not learnt backstroke. I had seen several older people who could float on their backs motionless for considerable periods. It, therefore, dawned on me that this was a challenge that I could undertake at my age. Lying flat on my back motionless would also enable me to relax.

I enrolled with a local pool for a course and paid the full course fees. I began the very next day. Unfortunately, the pool had no heating facility, and the water was ice cold! Even so, I jumped into the pool and did freestyle swimming for an hour. I felt happy about it. The backstroke lessons were scheduled for the succeeding several days. Unfortunately, my body could not withstand the exposure to cold water, and I fell ill almost immediately after the first day. I could not even get up the following morning. Although I felt sad and disappointed momentarily, this experience increased my resolve to succeed. I just had to make sure that I chose a heated pool that would prevent the cold exposure and give it a second chance.

After searching for a while, I found a heated pool that had superb ambiance and good coaching facilities. When I saw it, I was elated that it was an ultra-modern heated pool. Each course comprised of 20 hours, one hour at a time. I requested the lady who was in charge of the courses if I could do 40 lessons, 30 mins at a time. She made a special concession for me due to my age. I paid the full course money and was excited to start the following morning. I decided to go round to see all the available facilities. I climbed a few steps and tried opening what I thought was a door. It turned out it be a spare glass door that was just kept next to the regular one. I pulled it and suddenly it came off. I tried to hold it but it was heavy and I fell down with the heavy glass door shattering right on top of me. I got hurt badly on my hands. The lady in charge apologized stating it was their fault but the damage was done.

That was the second time that nature seemed to have conspired against my learning the backstroke!!! It did not deter me one bit. I requested and was allowed to start the lessons after full recovery. I thanked the lady in charge, for the accommodation she had made, rather than feeling angry and bitter about the experience. After about 8 or 10 days I was absolutely normal. I desired to start classes the following day. As was my habit, went to the nearby park in the evening for a four-mile walk. I had almost finished and only about 500 meters were left. I began to sprint. Unfortunately, I ran over a stone embedded in the loose mud and fell on my hands. I got badly injured. The skin on my inner left hand had fully come off. My elbow was sprained. I was rushed to the nearby hospital where the wound was dressed. I was also given a tetanus shot. Fortunately, I did not suffer a fracture. This was a third time that my plan for learning the back-stroke was thwarted. Again, I felt dejected and felt like crying. I started blaming my fate and luck and suddenly, I remembered the lessons that I learnt during my meditation classes.

After a short meditation, I was calm and collected and reasoned that upsets happen in life. It is at such times that our true personality reveals itself. All the yoga classes and meditation practice sessions that I had attended helped me to replace my negative thoughts about fate and lock into a strong positive mindset. Once more, I got back on my feet with a strong resolution that come what may, I should not quit. Once more, my resolve strengthened and there was no way I could quit. It took me over two weeks to get back into shape. Finally, I started classes with a schedule of 8 weeks of 5 sessions per week.

After just three lessons I was able to do backstroke and remain on my back on the water!!! A combination of determination, perseverance, and the will to overcome challenges helped me succeed. This accomplishment boosted my self-confidence and gave me immense satisfaction. Even at the age of 89, I could complete all the forty lessons in 8 weeks. I believe that the ambition to succeed, backed up by determination, will and perseverance has enabled me to climb the ladder of success step by step in many dimensions – from abject poverty in childhood to a reasonable wealth; from a weak physique to fitness; from a narrow upbringing to a global perspective in life; from a need to possess objects to the joy of giving them away; from anger and jealousy to calmness, positivity and a genuine appreciation of everyone around me; and from a struggling life to a purposeful one. With this transformation comes much happiness.

I find that challenging myself continuously to become better, to learn new skills, to engage in new pursuits, and to interact with new people is an important step on the road to happiness. Although I try to keep these challenges realistic, often stumble and fall (sometimes literally!!).

The important thing is to get up and go again, to try over and over again without losing patience, without blaming the others, and without getting too bogged down by the obstacles in the path.

d. Relationship with Family Members and Others

As I have said earlier, it is not merely enough to keep the relationship with family members and friends. It is important to cultivate and nurture the relationships, at the same time ensuring that you are never perceived as imposing on them. At every step of the way, one needs to be aware of the relationship and invest effort into evaluating and identifying the best way to improve the relationships.

For example, when my wife passed away, it was tempting for me to start living with my children whom I have always loved greatly. Moreover, they both wanted me to stay with them. They have both become extremely thoughtful and responsible individuals and I do not even have a scintilla of doubt that they would gladly take responsibility for caring for me. Staying with them would give me all the comforts in life. I would always have a nice room for myself in their houses. The staff in the house would do my bed and clean the room every day. All meals would be prepared and served nicely.

There was only one problem in the scenario. What would I do from morning to night? Nothing. How was I going to keep myself busy? My children and other family members are in the prime of their work lives and would have little time to spend with me even if they wanted to. They have their priorities, work, traveling, looking after their children, and so on (as they should). Very soon, I would have to spend time alone at home with just the helpers! How much could I read the newspapers and books, and watch television alone? Almost surely, I would be bored and start feeling lonely over time. The free time invites unwanted thoughts that often give rise to feelings of purposelessness. Idleness is the nemesis of happiness!! I realized after much thinking that the best way to remain happy was to lead an independent life at my own home. Ironically, far from making me lonely, staying alone has made me active and engaged with others. By being independent, I have avoided unintended and unwanted irritations and misunderstanding.

However, leading a happy life is a process that requires an investment of thought and effort. The first part of it is motivation. With my loving wife gone, at the age of 80 years, the motivation to live a happy life was very important. A little thought convinced me that it makes no sense to feel miserable for the rest of my life. The best tribute to my wife is to live a full and happy life in which I love others and help everyone as much as possible. Once I realized this, I was motivated to lead a full, active, and happy life.

The second part is to plan for happiness and execute the plan – just like any management or military exercise. I needed support at home for cooking and cleaning. I also needed a driver who could take me wherever I wanted to go. I devoted much thought to it and as I have mentioned elsewhere, I employed Nagu to cook and clean for me and Lokesh to drive me around. Over time, I have supported them, developed a good rapport with them, and have even started thinking of them as my own children. In turn, Nagu fully supports me by taking care of food, washing, dusting, staying at home and Lokesh is ever willing to take me out any time I want.

The third and perhaps the critical thing I did was to think, plan, and manage my relationships with my children, grandchildren, and friends. I thought about how I would feel if I did not receive calls or messages regularly from them. After much thought and experience, I have come to realize that it is not the frequency or the regularity of interaction but the quality of interaction that brings satisfaction and happiness. On my part, I feel and act in a way that makes them happy and in turn, it ensures my own happiness. It is important to realize that imposing on others in any way results in resentment and unhappy relationship. I have cultivated contentment in the way I think of, and interact with, my family members. I think of my family members in some context or the other almost daily. Although they are not in close physical proximity, I have been able to maintain a loving relationship with all my family members. Good family connections ensure that I never feel lonely. I emphasize that it is in our own control and requires molding the mind in a way that fosters the relationships.

Unfortunately, I know of several people who live together as a joint family but feel miserable most of the time. Why does this happen? My view is that physical proximity increases the need to be flexible and adjusting, for tolerating the idiosyncrasies of others. In fact, it becomes quite challenging to maintain a meaningful and happy relationship. On the other hand, a little distance goes a long way in allowing a more meaningful interaction. It is easier to develop such a relationship and make it happy. Yet, it is very important to think carefully and plan the interactions in a way that caters to the needs of everyone in the relationship and fosters love and understanding.

It does not happen overnight, and it is not automatic. Just because someone is closely related, it does not mean that they are obliged to love you!! You need to earn the love and understanding. I spend time with family but for short durations. I have made it a point to listen to the kids, express my appreciation liberally, and never judge them or offer unsolicited advice. I always praise them liberally, making both them and me feel good. I am always eager to learn from my grandkids. I have learnt many good things from them on technical subjects involving the internet, laptops, IPads, iPhones, and iPods. I seek their help if and when they are free. Even now, while I am editing this book on my laptop, I have often sought their help. I feel so blessed to have them around and so glad that they are eager and happy to share this knowledge with me. I feel that this is the way that human relationships are built. Not realizing this can only be a recipe for unhappy relationships.

After living on my own for the last 14 years I can say with confidence that this three-stage process – motivation, independence, and well-thought-out relationships - has worked beautifully for me. I feel younger, energetic, healthy, and cheerful even at the age of 94. My view is that you find happiness around you if you decide to be happy. Many people ask me how I manage to be cheerful, energetic, and active at my age. With humility, I can say that happiness is essentially an internal process of transforming your mind more than anything external to you. I feel physically fit and mentally agile every day. Not a day has passed in all these years that I can recount as not having total mental satisfaction. My love and affection towards my children and grandchildren have only grown. They talk about me to all their contacts whenever they meet.

I need to mention that while I am not financially strapped, I do not live an ostentatious life. Over the last 14 years, I have never had any issue of not having enough financial resources. My main expenditures are the payments to my caretaker Nagu and driver Lokesh. Nagu has become an expert cook and what she cooks is healthy and tasty. I eat whatever she cooks in small quantities. I realize that I do not have the same metabolism as younger people and therefore, I need to limit my food consumption to my bodily needs. I can no longer digest rich restaurant food. Therefore, I have limited the times that I eat out. I do not spend money on material possessions that I do not need – they no longer attract me. I concentrate on my wellbeing and happiness. Thus, I usually have more money than I need for the simple life that I am leading. I share it by donating for good causes. This habit of giving has also given me much satisfaction and happiness.

Almost everyone who interacts with me asks me about my zest for life. I wonder at times about the total transformation that I have undergone. I remember the earlier times when I was short-tempered and irritable, blamed others often, and even used bad language. I am so glad that I have grown spiritually, and I no longer feel the anger, the frustration, the irritation, and annoyance that marked my earlier life. I owe my transformation to the various spiritual teachers with whom I have interacted by doing yoga, meditation, and pranayama. Every day is a new opportunity to renew and learn, to love, and be loved. I savor the beauty and bounty of nature, feel the goodness of others, and enjoy every day. Happiness abounds in every moment that I am awake. I am so grateful for it.

My present commitment to write this (second) book is also part of what is giving me happiness. It makes me think, reflect, and introspect. It challenges me in articulating my own experiences in a way that I had never done before. I even dream about ways in which I can convey my experience to others who might be helped by it. In a practical sense, it has given me even more purpose in life. It leaves no time for idle gossip – so much the better. This is particularly challenging because I am not a professional writer and not used to articulating my thoughts in a way that others can grasp and presenting my experience in a way that helps them. But that is what I want to do, and I look upon this as another learning experience, another way of reaching out to those around me. As always, I feel grateful to have had this opportunity to write this book.

I find it important to invest and build relationships with others with mutual love, understanding, affection, and compassion where needed. No relationship – not even with your spouse and children – should be taken for granted. I find that love begets love and empathy begets understanding. Keeping expectations low – a willingness to give more but take less – is the key to building a good relationship. Good relationships are the essential building blocks of the edifice of happiness.

   e. **Adaptability**

For over a decade I have been following a set of routine in my daily tasks I get up at a particular time have morning coffee, read spiritual books, offer my prayer to the almighty and look at the newspaper or switch on the TV only afterwards. When I am at home, I follow a strict daily routine for my breakfast, lunch, and dinner. I have breakfast consisting only of fruits and a cup of black tea at 9 AM. I have a typically south Indian vegetarian lunch including a cup of yogurt at 1.30 PM.

Finally, I have my and dinner consisting of a bowl of salad, dal, and sabzi with two dry chapatis and a cup of yogurt at 8.30 PM. Rarely do I change this routine.

This routine completely changes when I visit my sons. I visit my elder son's house in India for short periods doing weekends when they are not traveling. When I visit my son in India, the food is quite different but normally I maintain the timings except when their friends visit them. It is common for the dinner to get pretty late. It does not bother me because I enjoy and become completely oblivious to the passage of time when I am meeting new and interesting people.

In contrast, I visit with my second son in the US for up to 6 months at a time. When I visit the U.S., I face a very different setting. Unlike in India where the maid spends every day at my older son's place, in the U.S., the maid comes once every two weeks to clean and dust the whole house. Because my daughter-in-law works part-time, she cooks the food for the whole week on only two days in a week: Thursdays and Sundays. Generally, at dinner time, we all gather as a family and eat together. Although the evening food that I eat in the US is typically vegetarian, it is very different from what I eat in India, but it is very tasty.

When I am in my son's place in Wilmington, DE, because both my son and daughter-in-law work, I am all alone from morning till about 7 PM but I never felt lonely. On the contrary, I keep myself very busy. I use the treadmill daily to keep myself fit. I take charge of their three lovely and adorable dogs, feeding and cleaning them at the appropriate times and taking them out for walks as well. In the evenings, whenever they are free, I also go out for walks with my son and daughter-in-law. I find it very refreshing and satisfying.

I make my own coffee and breakfast in the morning. Almost every day, I have a lunch consisting of a bagel with hummus and cheese, a vegetable burger with hot sauce, a glass of chilled unsweetened soya milk, and a fruit. I follow this routine for months starting from the time of my arrival till my departure from the U.S. Several people are quite surprised at the ease with which I change from the South Indian cuisine in my home to this Americanized cuisine when I come to the US. In all candor, I enjoy the change in food!! I lose about 7 pounds of weight during my visit to the US. I feel light, good, and energetic.

I also find that the perspectives on weight and food are different in India, which makes my friends and relatives feel that I look haggard when I return to India. Even my cook feels that way and advises me to eat more of her tasty food when I return!! I greatly appreciate the goodness of their hearts and the care and concern they bestow upon me that makes them say these nice things to me. After all, spending time with my loved ones including grandchildren is so much more satisfying and important for me than the food that I eat. This perspective – prioritizing the relationships and not negatively interpreting their care and concern – is what keeps me cheerful and happy. I never demand anything more than what they provide, while greatly appreciating all the closeness, care, and concern that they show me. When people advise you, it is not because they think negatively about you but because they care, and they think positively about you. You may follow their advice or discard it but do not discard the closeness that you can forge by appreciating why they care to advise you. That is what keeps me free of negative feelings and fosters happiness and health.

During my visit to the US, I fly alone to Dallas, Texas to spend nearly a month with a close family related to my wife. They love, admire, and respect me and treat me like their own father. I find total peace in their house - like being in a sanctuary. The husband is a university professor, and his wife gave up working to devote more time to reading and housekeeping. When I visit, she gives me a good company and takes loving care of me. She serves me a hot breakfast that includes oats, toast with eggs, and coffee. She prepares typically South Indian lunch but with less spice. Normally, I have a dinner that includes a big bowl of tasty salad, a chapati (similar to a tortilla), and vegetables. There is a mini gym at home, and I work out almost daily. I have also visited different locations with them during my visit to Dallas. I get much warmth from the love they bestow upon me and this gives me much happiness. After the visit, I feel rejuvenated and very cheerful.

Overall, my stay of nearly six months in the U.S. is filled with contentment and total happiness. I take my two granddaughters out for shopping and dining when they visit home from their colleges. They are very fond of me and it is indeed a bliss spending time with these lovely grandkids.

A key factor that cements our relationship during my visits is that I have learnt to say 'Yes' and never 'NO'. For example, whenever I am asked if I would join him/her/them for trail running, I readily agree. Likewise, I participate with them during walks, swimming, and other activities.

While I may not be very good at some of the activities, I always try to do my best, not to compete with others but to challenge myself to become better. This attitude of give-and-take has brought me very close not only to my family members, but also to friends' acquaintances, and neighbors. I make myself readily available to lend a helping hand without hesitation.

Adaptability to the context – the flexibility to change where needed – is essential for building relationships, and ultimately to be a happy person. While there is comfort in routine, recognizing that others might have different routines and adjusting my routine to conform to others has served me well in providing much happiness.

f. Pets

When I visit the U.S., I take care of the three dogs[10] with my son's family. Looking after these three pets is a labor of love. Just like little children, they are innocent and very endearing. As soon as they see me, they get highly excited and are so happy!! When they are with me, they are always trying to make me play with them. Playing with them for some time is a lot of fun and just like meditation, gives me total happiness. They also have an amazing sense of timing. How they sense the time is still a mystery to me. All the play stops when it is time for snacks around noon. Just about this time, Daisy, the oldest among them, starts barking at me to attract my attention. If I happen to be in my room with the door closed, she stands in front of the door and scratches the door while barking!! Initially, she barks a little to see if I get the message. If I ignore her, she starts barking louder. At some point, I succumb. Even then, she follows me closely to see what I am up to. If I take their food bowls, they all know that I am preparing their lunch and they immediately become very quiet. If I try doing something else, they all restart barking incessantly to attract my attention.

Once I start preparing their food, they become serious, stop barking, and stand quietly just behind me!! When I serve lunch, all three of them gulp down the food!! They lick the bowls clean to ensure that nothing is left! This whole experience is so nice and pleasant that it is almost therapeutic. I watch them finish their lunch and then take them to the basement to ease themselves. I clean up after them and then, I am completely free and undisturbed till the next meal!! They seem

---

[10] Unfortunately, even as I write this, I have learnt that Daisy, the oldest of the three dogs, has passed away. She is part of the family and has a special place in my heart. I grieve for her as I would for any family member. It is amazing how much peace and happiness the pets can give you.

to have better instincts than human beings. The most important part of interaction with the pets is that their love is so unconditional and their acceptance of you is so complete. With them, there is only love without judgment and loyalty without expectation. Like babies, they provide you with joy, happiness, warmth, and peace.

Pets often symbolize unconditional love. Experiencing such unconditional love can go a long way in providing an abundance of happiness. There is also a lesson that the pets teach us – give unconditional love to be loved back.

g. Expectations

They say that experience is a great teacher. The experience of poverty is an unforgiving teacher. From childhood, I learnt to share. Food and space were so scarce that we learnt to share equally without a second thought. This was a daily lesson that we imbibed from the time we were small children. I clearly remember the times when my siblings and I were between the ages of 5 to 9. Food was scarce and the only way we could get more food was to beg. We all learnt to eat less rather than beg. In retrospect but we permanently ingrained the lessons of sharing and contentment with what we have without desiring for what others have. I want to clarify that while we did not covet what others possessed, we all developed a burning ambition – an aspiration to be better and to lead a life without too much scarcity. We learnt to be content while working hard towards becoming better. We learnt to share and enjoy the warmth of giving. Most importantly, we learnt to not expect.

As a young boy, I would go begging to bring home whatever I could get from the kind-hearted people in town and I would then hand over the entire amount (or grains, etc. that some would give) to my mother. Meager though the amounts were, she would use them wisely to partly tide over severe shortages. Not once did she ever say a bad word about those that did not give. She taught me never to expect anything at all. Whatever people give, comes from the kindness of their hearts. We did not expect anything from even the closest of our relatives. If we had expected, almost sure we would have had disappointments and we would have permanently damaged our family relationships. It broke my heart as a child (and to this day, I feel a lump in my throat when I think of my mother) that in order to feed us and send us to school, my dearest mother suffered so much. Often, she would not even eat. It must have been a superhuman challenge to pay the fees and see us through high school. I remember the happiness, excitement, and elation that I felt when I got a job with a salary of Rs 30 a month!!! I was waiting eagerly for my first payday. As soon as I received my monthly pay in the form of 30 silver rupee coins, I literally ran home in excitement and gave it to my mother. She gave me a warm hug – one of the most memorable hugs I have ever received in my life.

Too much expectation is often the bane of life. Unrealistic expectations will almost certainly not get fulfilled and beget disappointment. Not just that, expectations from others that are not fulfilled lead to anger, frustration, and negative feelings about those who did not fulfill your expectations. In fact, expectations result in a spiraling growth of disappointment and anger. When you expect something from another person, your expectation may either be satisfied or not satisfied. If it is not satisfied, it results in immediate disappointment and anger. If it is satisfied, it is very likely that the next time, your expectations become higher!! As expectations become higher, the likelihood of disappointment also becomes higher. This is particularly true if the interactions tend to be repetitive.

Expectations from close relatives often result in this spiraling phenomenon, and ultimately could result in life-long loathing and enmity. Many times, when I was young, I wondered why my parents seldom asked their friends and families to help. Now I know the wisdom of not asking for help. In particular, asking and not getting the money destroys the self-esteem, and makes you feel embarrassed and highly resentful of the person who refused to give money. From childhood, I have learnt that blaming and faulting others, gets you nowhere other than to an unhappy world. Expectations kill happiness. Even between spouses, unrealistic and ever-increasing expectations can spiral out of control and result in continuous tension and even in a break-up of the marriage.

An essential element in the pursuit of happiness is managing expectations. Personal expectations can lead to a lot of pain, suffering, tension, and unhappiness in life. The closer the person is, the greater is the damage caused by unrealistic expectations. Expectations from even non-human systems could also lead to unhappiness. For example, an expectation of actions from a government that is not fulfilled can cause a loss of trust and much anger and frustration to you. It is a double whammy- what you wanted, did not take place to your satisfaction, and the anger and resentment you felt destroy your peace of mind.

CHAPTER 18

INDIVIDUALS AND FAMILIES WHO HAVE CONTRIBUTED TO MY HAPPINESS

Over the last 15 years, I can say candidly that I have enjoyed total bliss. I am truly grateful and feel blessed to have had some extraordinary relationships with people who have contributed immeasurably to my happiness. I mention a few of them below for helping me stay happy.

My neighbor, Mrs. Naomi Hass

I live in an apartment on the third floor of the building in Bangalore. My 78-year old neighbor, Mrs. Naomi Hass lives on the same floor, just three apartments removed from me. We have been neighbors for the last thirty years. A devout Roman Catholic, she is like an angel who has come down from heaven to help humanity. I have never heard her mentioning anything negative about anyone at any time during these thirty years. She is always there to help if anyone needs help.

Like her mother, Naomi's daughter Charmaine is an ever-smiling, all-positive ever-helpful, and charming person. After long years of courtship, she married a Hindu engineer from the state of Rajasthan but settled in Bangalore since childhood. They have a son, Aaryan. Their family is a lesson in harmony and love. For one thing, even though Charmaine was raised as a Roman Catholic, she and her husband have adjusted extremely well with each other. While she continues to pray at the Church, her husband is a keen student of the life of Saint Vivekananda. They learn from each other, respect and admire each other and live an admirable life of harmony and bliss. Naomi, Charmaine, and her family are not only good to each other but are so very helpful and good to everyone around them.

Naomi's husband Boney was likewise a remarkable human being. Boney and Naomi lived a very happy life but about two decades back, Boney fell very sick. Naomi nursed and cared for him and gave him great comfort and support during his last days. His death was traumatic for Naomi and caused her unbearable grief for a very long time. Charmaine and her family helped her cope with her loss and recover over time.

After my wife passed away, Naomi and Charmaine's family have been like a tower of strength for me. I feel immensely blessed and grateful for the love they have showered on me, and for the care that they have given me in times of need. I have never felt lonely with their family next door. Naomi introduces me to everyone as her best and only brother on earth!! I fully reciprocate the feeling and consider her as my best sister. We are all part of the same family!! Our friendship has blossomed and deepened over the years. Numerous acquaintances of mine know her and her family and are highly impressed by them. They inquire about Naomi and Charmaine without fail. We have become very close and fond of each other. When I travel abroad, the first call that I can expect is Naomi's!! We are in constant touch with each other wherever I am. She has, in a way, become my physical therapist! I have fallen several times while practicing for a marathon. Every time, she cleans and bandages my wounds, and cares for me like a real sister. I believe that her being there next to me has been an immense blessing for which I am ever grateful. In gratitude, I pray for the good of her and her family every single day.

My Family Members

I am truly blessed to have two sons, aged 61 and 56 years, who are both outstanding in their fields but at the same time, are extremely affectionate and loving towards me. They have two sons and two daughters. One stays in India and the other one in States. The older along with his wife are marketing and sales professionals. The younger one and his wife are both Doctors of Medicine and run their clinics. They are so busy with work and children. How can, even if they want, be with me always? It is not practical. Even more, my two daughters-in-law are truly angels. They are loving and affectionate towards me and compassionate and kind towards everyone. My elder son and daughter-in-law are in India (Bangalore) and my second son lives in Wilmington, Delaware. As I have mentioned elsewhere in this book, I visit both and when I am with them, I truly enjoy their company, their hospitality, their love, and affection.

I have four grandchildren, two sons of my elder son, and two daughters of my younger son. All four of them are very fond of me and I am very fond of all four of them. I savor the happiness of every moment that I spend with my grandchildren. Their activities and their achievements are truly a source of great happiness for me. My brothers' two daughters whom I brought up as my own daughters, are also very affectionate and loving towards me. They also view me as their dad, and I feel so grateful and so very happy that they and their families are doing fabulously well. My sister who is now 80 years old, lives just a few miles away. We like each other a lot. Although she has some health problems, her youngest daughter stays with her and attends to her needs. She too got widowed about two years back. Overall, I have an extremely cordial relationship with everyone in my close family – my sons, grandchildren, and my nieces, and my sister. With them and my neighbors, I have so far led a glorious life!! All of then are quite amazing in their love and gratitude towards me. They have given me much happiness and continue to do so.

Nidhi and Devi

Another family that I would like to mention is that of Bin Srinidhi (called Nidhi, for short, in the family) and his gentle wife, Shreedevi (called Devi, for short, in the family). Nidhi is my wife's cousin. My mother-in-law was the sister of Nidhi's father. I had little contact with Nidhi before May 1978 when he got married. His wedding was in Bangalore, and at that time, I was posted in Delhi which is roughly 1500 miles away. I was keen to get to know them better and this was an appropriate time. My wife and I took a flight from Delhi and landed at the place of the wedding, much to the surprise of many! Since then, we have come to like each other a lot.

Nidhi graduated with an undergraduate degree in electronics engineering from the Indian Institute of Technology, Madras, and then got his post-graduate degree in Business Administration from the Indian Institute of Management, Ahmedabad. Although he could easily have pursued a career with multinational corporations, he chose to join the Indian Administrative Service (IAS) for lower compensation. He was ranked 14th in the All-India Union Public Service Commission selection examination for IAS out of almost a million contestants (about 800 are selected every year to serve in different states in India)!! He worked briefly for two years as the Assistant Commissioner and Sub-divisional Magistrate in a place called Chitradurga in his own native state of Karnataka. He and his wife were both uncomfortable with the near-feudal culture in the service and the constant interference of local politicians in purely administrative decisions. While in the service, Nidhi took study leave to do his Ph.D. in Accounting at Colombia University in New York. After graduating in 1984, he resigned from the IAS and took up a tenure-track teaching position at New York University's Stern School of Business. Later, he taught for a time at Rutgers University in New Jersey and then moved to Hong Kong where he taught at the City University of Hong Kong and Hong Kong Polytechnic Universities. Devi got her undergraduate and post-graduate degrees in Pharmacy from Birla Institute of Technology and Science in Pilani near Delhi.

She worked for a time in the US in a pharmaceutical firm but then chose to look after their young daughter and take care of the house.

When Nidhi was teaching at Rutgers University in New Jersey, my second son moved to the US to pursue a residency at the Albert Einstein Medical Center at the Bronx in New York. Both he and his wife initially stayed with Nidhi and Devi in New Jersey for a short while before moving to an apartment at the medical center in the Bronx. During this time, they developed a close friendship. My wife and I visited them a couple of times when my son was doing his residency in New York. This was also the time when our relationship got cemented. Later, after my wife passed away, I contacted them when I was touring Hong Kong and they insisted on my staying with them. I spent a total of 20 days with them. We visited Macao Island also at this time as one family. I was lovingly looked after by them and I returned with a feeling of being in a retreat!! It helped that both were as health conscious as I was. We would go for long walks every day. I could also work out on the treadmill, stationary bike, and do exercises on the mat. This visit brought us much closer than before.

Both of them are a down-to-earth couple. They liked me as much as I liked them. They wanted me to visit them yearly for a month's stay. That was very nice of them. It was also obvious that they liked and greatly respected me. I was living alone and getting such an unexpected invitation made me so happy. I also wanted to visit them and have done so nearly every year. Both of them receive me at the airport every year with fruits and juices! They hosted a big birthday party for my 90th year!! I am so happy at being loved so much by them. I have come to treat them as my own children. During these visits, both in Hong Kong and in Dallas, I have gotten connected to several of their friends, mostly academics with considerable achievements but equally humble. They all call me Uncle! How gracious of them!! It seems that good people attract other good people and this is the best example. I treasure their love and affection. Even last year at age 93, I flew all by myself from Philadelphia to Dallas, a four and a half hour flight.

I have mentioned earlier about the marathon I ran in 2017 and launching my first book – an autobiography – in July 2017. I want to acknowledge the support I got from both Nidhi and Devi. They went through my original text in detail and made it more readable. Both would discuss the topics in the book and make alterations that they thought would improve the book. I am grateful to them for the time and effort they spent on the book. They have promised the same for this book as well. For the launch of the book in 2017, both flew in from Dallas to Wilmington, DE, and spent a few days with me and my son's family. They are marvelous people and have contributed in no small measure to my happiness.

CHAPTER 19

SELF-DISPOSSESSION AND GIVING TO OTHERS AS A CONDUIT FOR HAPPINESS AND SATISFACTION

The abject poverty and suffering I experienced (with my family) during my childhood have been a tough but great teacher. One of the lessons it has taught me is one of empathy. I feel the pain of other people who get stressed and are unhappy. It could be the death of a loved family member. Particularly, when the breadwinner is gone, the loss of financial resources can be daunting. The future looks bleak and the thought of going through stressful times due to poverty can be crushing. I can feel that pain. It has become part of me to reach out and help people in such dire situations both financially and in offering hope and support.

A case in point is my caretaker, Nagu. My wife and I employed her as a maid over 20 years ago when she was n her 20s. She had two young kids, a daughter, and a son. Her husband was an alcoholic and abusive philanderer who abandoned her for another woman. At that time, she looked emaciated and undernourished. She was depressed and saw no future. She agreed to work with us for a meager salary and was willing to work all seven days every week. All that she wanted was for us to provide her some food. My wife and I felt very sorry for her and allowed her to bring her kids also. Gradually, her energy came back, she glowed on her face and did not have that emancipated look anymore. She had a smile on her face that made us very happy. Now, 20 years later, she is like my daughter. She works with gusto and vigor. Her salary has been increased by manyfold. We supported both her kids to get an English medium education. Both cleared the high school and her daughter got admission to the university. After few months Nagu was keen to get her married. Our persuasion to allow her to complete her undergraduate degree was not enough to change Nagu's mind. We slowly understood that when it came to her daughter, we need to respect what she and her daughter decide, rather than forcing our views on them. We chose instead to bear the expenses of the marriage. Now. Nagu's daughter is happily married with two kids.

Nagu's son finally managed to get through high school after three attempts at the school completion examination but his performance was not adequate for him to get admission to a university. He also had no desire to go to university. In any case, Nagu is now self-sufficient. I bought her a small independent house with two bedrooms and a kitchen. However, she stays at my apartment and has rented out her house. She is extremely happy and has become a part of my family. I now consider her as my daughter. In my apartment, she has an independent room with a bath. It also has a television and is well furnished. She watches her local language programs. I am very happy that she is well settled and stays with me. I am quite confident that she will look after me as long as I live.

The other person that I have helped settle is my driver. I stopped driving and needed a driver after I lost my wife. Even for a younger person, navigating the traffic in Bangalore is quite a challenge. I did not want to take that risk. I was fortunate to find a very nice person, Lokesh, in his late twenties to be my driver. He joined me soon after my wife's passing. It is now nearly 15 years and he continues working for me happily. Initially, a few days after he became my driver, he started coming late for work. He blamed it on the non-availability of public buses on time. I immediately took him to a bicycle store and got him a new bicycle. I joked with him that I would not now accept a puncture of his bicycle wheel as an excuse for coming late!! He too laughed. Over the years I have supported him in many ways. Early in his employment, I financed him to buy two three-wheelers (also called auto-rikshaws). Three-wheelers constitute a very common means of public transportation in Bangalore. My only condition was that he should treat it as an interest-free loan rather than a gift and that I would adjust the amount in easy monthly installments against his salary. He was overjoyed by this arrangement. He rented out one of the vehicles and kept the other one for personal use. After he paid back the loan, I financed him again for two more three-wheelers under the same arrangement. Now he owns six auto-rickshaws. Has rented out five of them and has kept one for his own use. With this arrangement, his income increased fifteen-fold!!! He has also become financially highly responsible. He deposits all the surplus amount he gets and lives frugally. Five years ago, I decided to change my car to a bigger one. Initially, I thought of either selling or trading in my old car. It had done just 29000 miles and was in perfect running condition. Lokesh brought a customer who was willing to pay Rs 80000, a good sum of money. He had cared for my car nicely for over ten years. I felt that I did not need that extra money and decided not to sell the car. Instead, I thought of gifting the car to Lokesh. The only drawback was that I was not sure that he would keep it. No one in his family had a car. When I first suggested it to him, his first response was that he does not need a car. However, he thought about it and the following day, he was interested in my offer. Immediately, I signed all the required papers for transfer and within a week, Lokesh became the owner of the car. I felt extremely thrilled. He now has a bicycle, six autos, and an air-conditioned Maruthi Zen Car. I followed it up last year by helping him to lease a house on lease by gifting a major part of the lease amount. This was triggered by his having to vacate the place he was renting. The amazing thing was that he did not approach me – perhaps he felt quite embarrassed. By chance, I casually asked him about his rental place, and he mentioned that he was supposed to leave it soon. He had tried to locate an apartment close to my place but the rents in these areas were high. He could find a small place far away, but this would have made his commute consume far greater time besides the increased cost of gas. The owner of the rented place he was staying in, wanted a three-year lease but Lokesh found it beyond his capability to pay the large amount. After some thought, I finally made up my mind to pay a major portion of the money as a gift, knowing his pay-back capacity. With this arrangement, he is now comfortably settled for three more years.

Supporting these two individuals and seeing them become happy, comfortable, and prosperous has given me a deep sense of satisfaction. I often wonder about the transformation in myself!! I could never have dreamt of such acts earlier, coming out of poverty, struggling to enter college, and hoping for better (financially) times. More importantly, I have realized that true happiness lies in giving, not acquiring!! Genuine satisfaction arises from supporting those in need, consoling those in grief, and loving those who feel abandoned.

I have thought much about the counter-intuitive idea that it is dispossession, not possession, that helps in becoming happy. Financially, I have gradually cut down on my wants first and needs next. With my personal commitments slashed to the minimum, I save most of the money that I get as retirement income. It is important to note that I have not cut my consumption so that I could save – rather, I save because I don't need that personal consumption. I realize that this is a profound change from my earlier days when I was struggling to live. Now, even my savings lying in the bank, earning interest, seems quite irrelevant to my happiness. As part of this changed mindset, I have been contributing to educational nonprofit institutions. It has now become a habit for me to seek out those who are in need and try my best to alleviate their fears and anxiety by giving.

A shocking incident that reshaped my life and changed my mindset forever was the untimely death of my brother at the age of 49 due to a massive heart attack. As I have mentioned elsewhere, he left behind his young wife and two daughters aged 15 and 10 years, with no money in the bank, and no other savings other than an insurance policy for two lakh rupees. I had always looked upon him as my son and had financed his education up to and including a master's degree in physics. He was also very fond of me. I remember the relief and happiness on his face when I came back all the way from London when our father died in 1966. His death was so sudden and so shattering that I was very distraught. My feelings were compounded when I saw the condition of my sister-in-law. Suddenly, I felt nervous and uneasy. It was impossible for me to bid her goodbye and just leave. Deep in my heart, I felt the urge to ensure the future for my brother's wife and children just as he would have. My own comfort and ease of life would have mattered little if I abandoned my duty. I was so distraught that I spent the whole night crying and wondering what I could do to help them in their hour of need. I decided to take them with me and made myself a promise to look after them until they were able to stand on their own feet. My sister-in-law was relieved beyond belief and was immensely grateful that I was there to support her at this time. Although I could not consult my wife at that time, she was more than welcoming of all of us when we all landed at our place. Although I had acted without consulting her, she expressed an amazing understanding. She hugged all three of them, welcomed them to our family, and assured them that she would do everything to help all of them.

My wife and I decided to give up many of our comforts in our desire and dedication to support my brother's family and bring up his children as our own. It was the best decision that we made in our lives. They stayed with us for 12 years during which time they enlivened our life, and we were able to live as one big happy family. Caring for them as part of our own family completely altered our way of life for the better. We had no assets nor even a home of our own, and our income was limited. Yet, we had opened our hearts!! We never felt uneasy shouldering additional responsibilities. This experience taught us that the willingness to make others cheerful pays rich dividends in ways that we cannot even fathom. Both daughters of my brother completed their education, and both married wonderful persons and to this day, they are extremely happy and have wonderful families. My sister-in-law moved out after 12 years with us and stays with her elder daughter. It gives me immense satisfaction and extraordinary joy to see them happy, prosperous, and thriving.

Another instance that comes to mind is our supporting a relative stranger. The daughter of my son's professor got admitted to a college about 60 miles away from Bangalore. The parents were a little concerned about letting their daughter go to a place where they did not know anyone. They knew us casually as the parents of a student but having come to Bangalore, they paid a courtesy visit. When we met, they expressed their concern in a casual conversation. Without hesitation, my wife and I expressed our willingness to look after her. During her five years of study, she visited us frequently. She was a very sweet person, and it is no exaggeration when we say that we loved her so much and treated her as our own daughter. Even after 20 years, she is in regular touch and visits us.

These are some of the instances where we have extended ourselves to bring comfort to others. We learnt never to think of "self" as "I". Including others in the concept of self brings about immeasurable happiness.

CHAPTER 20

SELF-RELIANCE IS AN ESSENTIAL INGREDIENT OF HAPPINESS

An aspect of happiness that I have realized by experience is that independence and self-reliance contribute much to a happy life. I understand that there are circumstances in life when this is not possible. These circumstances could be either temporary or permanent. I realize that when such a condition is a permanent one such as physical disability, it is not possible to be fully self-reliant. However, often, independence is a choice – and it is sometimes tempting to choose to be dependent on your children or relative or someone else. That is the situation that I found myself at the time of my wife's demise. She had managed my household almost single-handedly for a very long time. My sons and daughters-in-law were more than willing to have me move into their homes. I knew that if I moved in, there would be no need for me to do any of the household chores and it seemed like an easy option. It was very tempting, especially at that time when I had just lost my life partner, to accept the offers.

Yet, I was not sure that it would be the best option. What if I continued to stay at my place and learn to manage the household? I was nearly 80 years old but was in good physical condition. It occurred to me that living independently would contribute to my peace of mind, happiness, and satisfaction. There were two potential drawbacks. The first was whether I could manage the household independently. The second was that I was getting on in years and how I could handle the ups and downs going forward. I banished the negative thoughts and started thinking about how I could become self-reliant and lead an independent life while being close to my children and their families. I should try it out at least.

It was obvious to me that I needed outside help to manage cooking, washing, and cleaning. Fortunately, Nagu was working as a maid taking care of washing and cleaning on a part-time basis. She never cooked herself but often helped my wife when she cooked. I talked to her about staying in my apartment and taking charge of all the household chores. I agreed to increase her salary besides providing all her daily needs including food, toiletries, and the like. She was very happy to accept this. She moved in and started carrying out all the household chores including cooking.

The food she cooked tasted very similar to my wife's cooking. This took care of a major part of household management. I was not very comfortable driving in the traffic of the city, particularly at the age of 80 and decided that I should get a driver who could drive me for shopping and other activities that I might become interested in. I looked around and as I have mentioned elsewhere, employed Lokesh. I really liked him from the beginning because he was always smiling and pleasant mannered. He also turned out to be a good handyman. For the last 14 years, he has not only taken care of the car and its maintenance but also many household work like changing the fused electric bulbs, minor woodwork routine cleaning, and dusting in the house. Nagu and Lokesh also are friendly to each other and work together. Between the two of them, they keep the whole house tidy. I am grateful to them for a myriad of small things - there are instances when I found the doors and or steel cupboard locked but could not locate the key. Lokesh would search all over to find it. I realize their value when they take even a day off!! Their taking care of the household chores frees up my time for everything that I need to do from meditation and walks to booking tickets for my travel, attending music concerts, managing my financial accounts, etc. It has freed up my time to learn new things, become familiar with new technologies, and doing other creative things. I have downloaded many apps, and regularly watch interesting programs on YouTube, watch movies and serials, listen to a variety of music - western, Carnatic, Sufi Arabian, and Chinese. These keep me happily engaged throughout the day.

    Traveling is an activity where it is difficult to find someone to accompany me most of the time. Even at my age, I travel independently. Independent traveling has boosted my self-esteem and confidence that I am able to do things myself. Moreover, I have met very interesting people during my travel and people – complete strangers – have been extremely nice to me. After my wife's passing, I have traveled by myself to Singapore, Malaysia, Bangkok, Hong Kong, and the United States. I have traveled yearly to the U.S. from India and inside the U.S. to Dallas, TX, Chicago, Los Angeles, San Francisco, Florida. I intend to continue this as long as I can.

    Living and traveling independently, ironically, has brought my children and grandchildren very close to me. We treasure the times when we meet. When I visit my children and grandchildren and spend a few days together, we all have a lot of fun, the time passes quickly, and we recollect those moments later and enjoy the memories!! I am almost certain that if I had lived with them, the intimacy and the closeness would have been *less*, not more.

If you have the opportunity to be independent, it is often better to seize that opportunity. It may seem ironic but is often the case that the more independent you are, the closer you become to your children and grandchildren. Independent living improves self-esteem, gives you confidence, and improves relationships. Of course, you also get privacy and the freedom to spend your time as you please.

CHAPTER 21

EGO IS THE NEMESIS OF HAPPINESS

My memory goes back to over 85 years ago when I was a young 9-year-old. The ancestral home where we lived, shared with my uncle's family, had two small rooms, a big kitchen (which we were not allowed to use), and another tiny room with no windows. This tiny window-less room became our kitchen, bedroom, and living room, all in one. It was a dark and dingy room with no aeration – used as the kitchen when mom cooked, living room during the rest of the day, and bedroom during the night. We were 9 people at home when my father was with us. Of course, we had no bedding - we just spread our linen and slept where we could. The room was infested with bugs, which would become active as soon as the only light – a kerosene lamp - was switched off. We had no electricity. Thanks to the bugs, heat, and humidity, we all were restless most of the nights. Our life was confined to this room. Life was a struggle and the suffering was palpable but we could bear all this suffering in silence or rather, we would have borne all this suffering but for our grandma who faulted us all the time.

Grandma lived in the same house in the other room with an uncle and his family who were relatively better off than we were. Because we were extremely poor, she could not bear the sight of us. Every morning, she would curse us as if we chose our poverty. She faulted us for every little thing with loud outbursts. She used the only relatively large kitchen that the house had to cook and feed our uncle's family. We were not allowed to use that kitchen. My mom was forced to cook for us in our small room which had no windows. We also had to get whatever wood we could from outside to light the fire and cook. Naturally, this resulted in a lot of smoke that would invariably envelop the whole house. For the life of me, I cannot figure out what else we could have done under the circumstances. But granny would not hear of any reason and would keep yelling at my mom and all of us the whole day. She wished that we all disappear. My mom would never raise her voice but was reduced to tears every day. We were little children and too afraid to protest. Moreover, we knew that the same grandma would be extremely nice and polite to my uncle, her younger son. The only reason for this explicit and intentional discrimination that I can think of is that my uncle and his family were relatively financially better off.

I suppose that grandma felt superior and ill-treated us because she could. She knew that we could not afford to go out and find another place to live and perhaps she got some pleasure ill-treating us. However, whenever she was not well, my grandma would suddenly transform herself into a gentle person and talk nicely to my mom!! My poor mother was so kind-hearted and compassionate that she would never hold a grudge and took care of grandma as well as she could. She had a heart of gold. She was a living example of gentility and never even complained about the obvious unfair treatment that she was getting. This whole experience was a great lesson for all of us. My mother showed us the way to deal with any frustration that we could have. Ultimately, gentility prevails over viciousness. *The meek shall inherit the earth!!*

In retrospect, I have tried to analyze and understand the dynamics of my grandma's hatred towards us. Her husband died suddenly leaving her with 10 kids and no money but plenty of liability. This made her restless and perhaps broke her spirit. She developed a visceral hatred of poverty and anyone poor. She was also highly diabetic and had other issues of health. She died because of complications arising from her diabetes. Her frustrations and diatribes were manifestations of the harsh conditions that she faced in life. She needed to vent it out and found my poor mother as the person on whom she could vent without any retribution. As we became older and moved on in life, I have often felt a little guilty of having hated her when I was a child. It is simply that we did not have the ability to understand life and forgive her. Many times, I think of her and feel bad that life turned out to be so bitter for her to the end. I pray for forgiveness at not having understood her from her point of view.

In due course of time, our financial condition improved, and our uncle moved to a new house leaving the old house to us. Even though we were now better off, I have learnt the importance and value of helping others in distress. Although our grandma's behavior brought so much grief and unhappiness to all of us, I learnt never to look down on those who were struggling to survive. On the contrary, I feel that it is my duty to help those in need. To this day, I have continued to practice this. There were times when we feared the recipients might feel that we were showing off. I have learnt that it is important to serve others while overcoming the feeling that they might resent it. Interestingly, all this has been ingrained in my two sons as well. They are both extremely generous, conduct many charitable activities, and are imbibed with the habit of giving.

CHAPTER 22

BRAIN GAMES AND KEEPING MYSELF MENTALLY ACTIVE
- EXAMPLE OF SUDOKU -

While being physically active is an important component of being happy, I hasten to add that mental activity is equally important. I have come to realize that only an active mind can achieve the balance necessary to be happy. The need for consciously keeping the mind active becomes more imperative as you age. I have seen many people, particularly those who have lost their life partners, losing interest in life, and doing almost nothing to keep their mind active. They often find it difficult to adjust to the reality that they have to manage life on their own. They often take the easy path, especially if they have someone to care for them. Although this appears good at the outset, it creates a multitude of problems. Often, they lose the sense of purpose in life and lead a pedantic and mechanical life, waiting for their timely feeds! The caretakers, even if they are their own children, have other responsibilities and priorities - towards their own family, children, and work. It is difficult for an elderly dependent parent to keep the expectations down at a realistic level from his or her own children. This creates misunderstandings and conflicts, ultimately resulting in misery for both. Getting into a dependent situation thwarts the motivation to take charge of your own life, define a purpose, and work towards it. Second, I have seen many dependent parents become lazy and complacent, with very little physical activity and almost no mental activity. Just as the body deteriorates without a conscious practice of health and fitness routine, the mind deteriorates in the absence of challenging activity. It seems to be a vicious circle and to be happy, one needs to break out of it.

What exactly does "taking charge of life" mean? What does independence mean? These are questions that need to be answered carefully in the context of an elderly person. In my case, I am in a healthy condition and if I decide to go out for a walk, I would not wait for too long to find a company!! I would go out of myself. Whatever I feel the need to do something, if I can do it myself, I will. If it is something that I cannot do or simply decide not to do as a daily chore (like cooking and cleaning), I seek outside help but that does not compromise my independence. If I were to wait every time for someone to accompany me on my walks, I would not be able to take the walk most of the time. Even when my own children accompany me for a walk, they might do so grudgingly as an obligation, or they might have work that makes them feel jittery while they fulfill their "obligation" This is not exactly a recipe for happiness!! This is a simple example of how independence becomes an essential part of achieving happiness.

There are two essential dimensions involved to take charge of one's life and be independent. The first is the physical dimension. One needs to consciously practice healthful habits in the food that one consumes and to be regular and disciplined in eating. In addition to healthful eating habits, it is important to maintain physical fitness through yoga, walking, and playing games that are appropriate for one's age and the state of health. Add to this mix the need to be physically active. All these lifestyle changes constitute the physical dimension. The second equally important dimension is the mental dimension. Practicing meditation, breathing exercises, and positive thinking need to be consciously cultivated to maintain mental balance. Keeping the mind occupied and active throughout the day is also essential. Those with a passion for any particular subject – say history or science or literature – could focus on reading, watching programs related to the topics of interest, and keep the mind active that way. Alternatively, those with a flair for playing games could keep their mind active by playing games such as chess, bridge, other card games, and solving puzzles. Those with a passion for philosophy could pursue nuanced philosophical thoughts and those who are religiously oriented could keep pursuing religious thoughts. All these contribute to mental activity and help in achieving and sustaining happiness. The things that often occupy the mind – and I think should be avoided at all costs - are gossiping, fault finding, and comparing with others. Gossiping is often judgmental talk about someone outside the circle and often achieves no benefits but could generate negative thoughts and slowly poison the mind. Similarly, fault finding is an exercise of developing and sustaining negative thoughts about someone else.

The absence or suppression of mental activity often lands people into depression, dementia, or some mental deficiency. Unfortunately, Alzheimer's, a form of dementia saps a person's life and spirit bit by bit till they become so demented that they are unable to recognize their own children. They need 24/7 assistance to perform daily chores such as eating or bathing. They need to be kept under vigilance all the time especially at night. I have heard of cases when they get up from their beds at night, go outside, and get lost. It becomes a problem that leaves the family devastated, burdened with the need for constant vigilance that is so difficult to sustain over a long period of time. While Alzheimer's is an extreme case, even casual loss of memory with old age leaves the elderly dependent on their children's families and could be the cause of much annoyance, embarrassment, and frustration. Love and affection are eroded and ultimately, the elderly are seen as burdens – so much so that their departure is greeted with a great sense of relief!!

I realized that with my determination to live all alone, I should ensure that I remain alert, happy, and conscious all the time. As I mentioned earlier in this book, I am blessed with having Nagu at home to take care of me and Lokesh to drive me around. I am grateful to both of them for taking care of my physical needs. I keep myself physically very fit with a healthy diet, regular exercise, and the discipline to be focused on maintaining my health and fitness. But that is not enough. I need to keep my mind active, keep exercising my memory, and challenge myself mentally just like I do physically. There are several games of skill such as chess, bridge, and some other card games. I could challenge my mind with crossword and similar puzzles. I tried many of these and found that I really like solving sudoku problems. I initially started with easy ones in the daily newspapers to familiarize myself with the puzzle. I have now progressed through easy, medium, hard, and hardest. I challenge myself and solve one "devilishly hard" sudoku puzzle every day. An important part of the challenge is that there are no easy thumb rules to solve the problem. I think a lot before starting and start with the most difficult part. At times I succeed in my first attempt. But there are times I need to try several times. Very rarely do I give up but that also has happened – but very infrequently. I find that it is important to continuously exercise the mind and keep thinking. I sometimes carry this thought process through the night. The happiness that I get when I solve a difficult puzzle is indescribable!! It is somewhat similar to the feeling I got when I learnt to do backstroke swimming at age 89!! The moral is to keep your brain working and this with intellect will keep you steady ensuring normal behavior. While I focus on puzzles like Sudoku, different people might find different avenues of interest. The underlying purpose, however, is the same. Keep the mind active and challenge yourself all the time. Never let it slip.

CHAPTER 23

DO NOT FIGHT TECHNOLOGY, EMBRACE IT USE IT TO YOUR ADVANTAGE!! *KEEP LEARNING*

All of us now are in an age where increasingly more technical devices have become part of our lives. Given that a large proportion of people routinely use computing and other technical devices routinely, they have become part of life and many things that used to be done manually and many other things that could not be done easily are now being done with these devices. To the extent that one is not part of this technological revolution, it becomes difficult and inconvenient for others to interact with that person. Consider someone who does not use any social media – no WhatsApp, no FaceTime, and no email. It imposes a cost on others to interact and over time, it becomes an annoyance.

In this day and age, having basic computer knowledge is almost as important as knowing addition or being literate. I got introduced to computers more than 25 years ago. People had started using desk computers to send and receive messages. I was curious and contacted an individual who was assembling and selling computers. On his advice I got one installed at home. He also explained the basics of how it works. I got him to install an internet connection. I learnt to communicate using emails. The devices were changing and improving rapidly, and Apple came up with devices that were much easier and handy to use for someone like me. I bought an iPad for myself and after a few years, I upgraded it to an iPad pro. Things started changing further with the introduction of smartphones and other mobile devices. I use an Apple iPhone. I have made it a point to read through the service manuals and experiment with the devices on my own. Slowly, I feel confident using these devices. With the help of a friend who is well versed with technology, I have learnt to load and delete music on my iPhone. I am also getting fairly confident in using the cloud to store music and other files so that I could download them on any device. I have saved over half a million classical songs and music that is accessible on my iPhone and iPad. I have also saved much of my music in the memory of these devices so that I can still hear my music when the internet is down, or I am at a place that does not have Wi-Fi. I have saved lots of information such as contact numbers, birthdays of relatives and friends, email ids, books on kindle, and documents. I have learnt to use Microsoft Word. I am also using social media such as Facebook and WhatsApp to share photos and videos. I am fairly confident in using Dropbox and Google cloud. On average I spend up to four to five hours per day on these gadgets. I watch and listen to spiritual meditation videos on YouTube on smart TV.

I have realized that the internet is going to change the world in ways that we have scarcely begun to understand. Even at my age, I use Google and Wikipedia to search for information on several subjects ranging from my prescription medicines to the shoes that I want to buy!! Google search enables me to see the pros and cons of medicines that are prescribed and how they work to treat the conditions I might have. I watch sports events from all over the world on my devices. I watch movies and episodes of interesting serials that have been produced on my TV at home while relaxing with a drink!!! I have a friend who sends full live concert videos through dropbox on the same day that the concert is held. I generally spend around 6 months in the United States with my son and his family. All the stored music comes handy to listen to, keeping me happily engaged. In addition, several music channels are available at the touch of a button. Using these facilities at ease has also boosted my self-confidence. I feel blessed to be alive at this age of technological marvel that makes it so easy for me to be informed about all the things that I need and be entertained in ways that I want!!

As we speak, I am writing this second book on my laptop using Microsoft Word at my age of just 94!!! If I could do it, almost surely most others can, too. It is important to keep one's mind open and learn. With the proper attitude, anything is possible for a person who is willing to put the effort. This keeps the mind active and productive, and in turn, provides immense satisfaction and happiness. As long as I keep learning new things, I feel much younger physically and mentally.
Keeping an open mind, learning and growing, embracing positive change – are all harbingers of happiness. There is no age at which you want to stop learning. It has made me feel young and energetic even at my age.

CHAPTER 24

THE MIND IS MORE POWERFUL THAN THE BODY
- A STORY OF DISCIPLINE AND DETERMINATION -

The concept of remaining physically fit and agile while keeping the mind focused and balanced, never occurred to me during the early part of my life. That was a time when we were struggling to get two square meals a day, sometimes succeeding and sometimes failing. When you are hungry and uncertain about the next meal, all that you can think of is food. Physical fitness and mental wellbeing appear as distant and abstract concepts.

I consider myself very lucky to have been selected to undergo training at the Indian Military Academy with orders to join on February 18th, 1946. Without this opening, I would have most likely ended my career as a clerk in a remote government office, retiring at the age of 55. I think about how life would be. Some others who did not get the opportunities that I did, continued to stay in the village and had many kids without a clue on how and where to educate them. I also think that I would have had a much smaller life span. These thoughts invariably lead me to remember with gratitude, the blessings of the almighty, my parents, and other well-wishers.

Looking back, the training at the academy involved both physical and mental aspects. Perhaps due to conscription, we were lucky to be instructed by highly qualified professors who were not only outstanding but also very courteous and friendly. We listened to lectures on English, mathematics, military history, citizenship, and basic science. To me, who just had a high school diploma, this was a God-given gift. It inculcated in me a desire and motivation for life-long learning.

I consider myself also very lucky, to have received extraordinary physical training. Every part of the body was exercised so that we would be in a very fit condition. We had to run long distances nonstop, clear obstacle courses, practice rope climbing, work out on parallel bars, learn to swim, ride horses, and play football, field hockey, basketball, volleyball, and squash. The 23-month training prior to commissioning, not only instilled discipline and regularity that would serve me throughout my life but also infused me with energy that comes only when you are very fit. At that time, I had very little appreciation of this kind of rigor in physical training. Only after passing out of the academy in Dec. 1947 and I got the rank of second lieutenant, did I realize the benefits of physical fitness. The lack of physical fitness in my pre-academy life made the training at the academy so much more difficult for me. I remember that difficulty, which serves me as a reminder of the need to keep myself healthy and fit. As I mention elsewhere, health and fitness are very important in leading a happy life.

I never really gave up my exercise regimen over the last 70 years. My bodily fitness and enthusiasm for life, have enabled me to strive for happiness in a disciplined manner. While under training at the academy, I had been trained for long-distance walks and runs. I remember our marching over the Siwalik mountain ranges for nine days and nights continuously. We covered a distance of 157 miles!! This one walk was enough to flatten the pot belly I had before!! With the walks and runs, and with the rigorous exercise regimen, my muscles became stronger and I became fit. After that, I have always striven to maintain fitness – never to go back to the pre-academy life. In 2002, while I was in the United States, my second son, Vinny ran the tough Marine Corps Marathon in Washington, DC. covering a distance of 26.2 miles. My wife and I were there from the beginning until completion. My heart swelled with pride at his achievement. In my parents' family, no one gave enough importance to health and fitness. I believe that as a result, many of them died relatively young. I was so glad that my son did. Despite a very tight schedule as a physician, he made it a point to run regularly. He has completed half-marathons and full marathons multiple times. In the last two years, he has completed some fifty milers and finally a 100-mile-long ultra-marathon in 29 hours under sub-zero temperature. I am also very grateful that his wife and daughters (my granddaughters) have supported him all the way and they too have completed full marathons several times. They all keep themselves fit with exercises, running, and meditation.

Every year since my son went to the U.S., I have been visiting them every year for nearly six months. After my son completed the marathon, I felt motivated to take this up as a challenge!! I was 84 years and had to make sure it was safe to run at least a half-marathon. I consulted with my doctors in India. They advised me against doing it at this age. If I was so determined, they wanted to get my heart tested first with an ECG and echocardiogram. However, my son who was a physician himself, was ecstatic when I told him that I wanted to run a half-marathon. He was highly encouraging and supportive of my intention. He assured me that I was in perfect health and immediately enrolled me for a half-marathon that was to take place on May 14, 2010. I had just completed my 84th birthday on February 27th. His support and encouragement, together with his immediate action in enrolling me, gave an immense boost to my confidence. I felt the excitement and thrill of doing it running through my veins!! I knew that most people at the age of 84 would balk at long-distance running, let alone initiate it at that age!! However, I was determined to do it.

The next step was to plan and act on the needed preparations for the half-marathon. With my son's help, I drew up a rigorous six-week training schedule. I started on the schedule the very next day. The schedule involved 6 days of training with a break on the seventh day – repeated every week. The distance to be run was ramped up from 12 miles in the first week to 40 miles in the 6th week!!! This was complemented by a schedule of body-loosening exercises. It is an understatement to say that it was tough. However, there were two compensating aspects of this project. The first is that it gave me a goal to be achieved in six weeks. Setting up a goal and working my way towards it helped me focus my body and mind towards a tangible objective. The second aspect was my determination to do so. Every week that I completed not only boosted my confidence but also strengthened my determination. This project gave me mental happiness that was beyond my wildest expectations.

By the scheduled date, I felt fitter than I had over a long time. It was also tinged with curiosity and concern because I had not done it before, and I could not know what unanticipated issues might come up. I started the race at a slow pace while most other participants overtook me. I was the oldest runner in the race and several of my competitors were in their 20s !! I followed my son's advice to start slowly and then pick up speed gradually. As I did so, I was surprised to see quite a few runners, those much younger than me, just giving up!! I was in good shape and finished 12 of the 13.1 miles in three hours at a speed of 4 miles per hour! I sprinted the remaining distance of 1.1 miles and finished the half-marathon in 3 hours and 11 minutes. It was tough and tiring but when I crossed the finishing line, I was surprised to see a young smart lady ready to a medal round my neck! Several spectators including my family members took my pictures. I was curious about all this and was told that I had run the fastest in my age category (age 70 and above). I was also awarded an inscribed beautiful trophy. I was so excited that I ran around happily with the trophy in my hand. The whole experience was truly exhilarating!! Although it was a little tough, the fact that I could complete it made me much happiness and satisfaction. It also motivated me to repeat it year after year.

During this first race, the weather was cool and partly cloudy. I was lucky because it had rained throughout the previous day and did not rain during the run. On my third race at age 86, the day started with a heavy downpour accompanied by chilly winds. It was very cold as I was just wearing a thin tee shirt and shorts. Several runners had covered themselves with plastic raincoats. I too had one but decided against wearing it. Running with this would be troublesome. After about an hour into the race, the rain stopped. We were drenched but felt good. By the time we finished the race, it was fully dry. The wet surfaces were slippery at times. I had to be very careful and keep my eyes focused on the ground. All this slowed me down quite a bit, but I was pleasantly surprised that here too, I received the first prize. I participated every year and completed seven races with three first and two second prizes. The last one was at the age of 91!! I finished it without any hindrance. Though I completed the race faster than most people, I was not awarded a trophy because I was clubbed with all runners who were 70 years old and over. I was least perturbed because I was not running for a trophy. For me finishing the was the most important achievement. The only race where I faced a real issue out the seven was the one at age 90. It was my sixth race and I had a desire to create a record. I started the race fine but just after three miles into the race, I started feeling a severe pain around my left thigh. I could hardly move. With ten more miles to be covered, I nearly lost my confidence. But my son, who was with me, guided me step by step till the finishing line. I took pain killers to subdue the intensity of the pain. My determination and grit overcame bodily pain. For me, this was the most memorable race. I carried on with extraordinary effort under excruciating pain *but never gave up.* Surprisingly, after the race, I hardly felt the discomfort!!

After this event, tried to introspect - to understand how I could manage to run in pain and still finish. Looking back, I cannot believe that I did it. I cannot even imagine how I did it. I believe that some unknown power must have guided me through the experience. The easy path would have been to give up and later reconcile and regret. I cannot say what made me take the harder path – to finish it and rejoice. I am convinced more than ever, that for a person who is determined and willing, nothing is impossible. *This particular race taught me the power of determination, the power of mind over body. The true strength of an individual is not in his muscles. It is in his mind.*

This race also taught me the gratefulness and its power of healing. I am grateful to my son for helping me at this time, grateful for all those who wished me well, and grateful for those who silently prayed for me.

That said, some things can make you rethink your plan. I wanted to continue running in marathons till the age of 100 or as long as I live. This plan has suffered a temporary setback. Two months after my seventh half-marathon at the age of 91, I developed a case of severe vertigo. I took all precautions as advised by the physiotherapist but even now, after three years, the imbalance remains, although with diminished intensity. Along with that, I also started experiencing severe pain at the hip after just a few minutes after I started walking. The orthopedic surgeon who examined me asked me to keep walking, nevertheless. I have been prescribed some medications to be taken daily. Yet, to remain fit, I began taking short walks multiple times a day. Also maintaining my routine of doing yoga while avoiding forward bending exercises. I have also bought a state-of-the-art treadmill to walk inside the house in a protected environment. I walk on it every day without fail. Once a week, I walk for more than an hour. I realize that I am doing less that what I used to. I accept it and I am grateful for what I can do. I feel blessed to be able to do what I can. I am still very hopeful of reverting to a more active lifestyle shortly.

CHAPTER 25

- THE TRANSFORMATION OF MY LIFE -
LEAD ME FROM DARKNESS TO LIGHT, FROM IGNORANCE TO KNOWLEDGE, FROM MORTALITY TO IMMORTALITY

Everyone seeks everlasting happiness and peace. However, happiness is neither an object that can be acquired nor is it an event – a switch that you can turn on. Happiness arises from a conscious investment of effort, a continuous orientation of the mind, and the discipline and willingness to change one's lifestyle. Happiness is the process itself, not the end of the process. I call it a process of re-engineering the mind and the body, a process that does not stop. In my view of things, it is not possible to find ultimate happiness – a nirvana – after which one can stop the process. There are no short-cuts, no quick fixes. I realize that some people might have to work harder to transform their lives than others.

The good news is that most people are wired for happiness. An obvious example is that of a child. A child is unencumbered either by the burdens of the past or concerns about the future. She lives in the current moment and is constantly learning from the experiences around her. Never have I seen a child give up learning in frustration!! When she learns to walk, she may fall a hundred times, but she picks herself up every time and tries to walk again. Finally, she learns to walk. When she learns to talk, she does not get the words, the diction, and grammar all at once. She tries and fails but is neither embarrassed nor frustrated by the failures. She does not get disappointed with herself, never loses hope, and never complains about the floor she is trying to walk on or the reaction of others to her talk. She has no fear of failure that allows her to truly rejoice in her success. She does not judge and could not care less about being judged. She neither thinks that the world is complex nor that it is simple. She does not think about it at all. She tries her best to adapt to the world and rarely tries to change the world. That is how we all started.

Over time, as we grow up, the experience of the world around us starts to weigh on us. We often train our mind to be unhappy. We mistakenly seek happiness in the objects around us. We start believing that a good house, a nice car, a great spouse, a nice meal, a refreshing drink – all objects of pleasure – lead us to happiness. Sometimes we get what we desire and sometimes we don't. When we get what we desire, we have the pleasure of having it for some time and then desire for the next thing. Desires grow continuously and in this endless cycle of desires, we experience more unhappiness than happiness. We mistake short-term pleasure for happiness. Surprisingly, most of us do not learn from our experience of not deriving happiness from objects. We sometimes seek happiness in others' recognition of our worth and feel dejected if that recognition does not materialize. Sometimes, we even get angry that such recognition was denied to us. In all these cases, unlike the child that was happy without seeking it, we judge ourselves and judge others, give up without trying enough, feel jealous of others who possess material objects and outside recognition, and feel the inadequacies and frustrations that naturally accompany these feelings. Then we wonder why we are not happy!!!

The greatest realization that I had was that happiness is right inside of me. I can change for the better, the ability to reform myself, the ability to learn, and the ability to introspect. It requires inward-looking, praying, and deep thinking. I have slowly come to realize that truly happy people choose a journey and a path that is unencumbered by desires, material objects, and outside recognition. I have come to understand in some measure the wisdom and the message communicated to us by the saints, the purpose of meditation, and the need for balance in life that comes with the practice of yoga. I have come to realize that sadly, most people create hell for themselves with the tools that they have been provided to create heaven.

The story of Siddhartha Gauthama, a prince of the Sakya clan, is instructive. Born a prince and surrounded by opulence, he saw unhappiness both inside and outside his palace. All the riches, all the recognition, all the respect and submissiveness of others, still could not make the young prince happy. In fact, they all seemed to make him miserable. His first realization was that this was not the real truth, certainly not the way to achieve happiness. He had the discipline and the determination to renounce his princedom with all its accompanying glory, the riches, and the servants. He even renounced his own family and set out in a quest for the ultimate truth. He realized the futility of ego, the emptiness of material comforts, and the hollowness of external recognition. Very simply, he realized that expectations lead to disappointments and happiness. Happiness had to come from inside. His realization was the true wisdom, and he was given the title of the Buddha, the one who has attained "Bodhi", the ultimate wisdom.

The story of the Buddha is illustrative. He came to a village to spread his message and was confronted by a skeptic who berated him as a fake purveyor of false promises. The Buddha listened to him calmly and at the end, requested him whether he could ask a question. The skeptic agreed. The Buddha asked him that if he got a gift for someone but if that person refused, to whom would that gift belong. The skeptic laughed and replied, "to me of course". The Buddha told him "Sir, you brought me a gift that you tried to give. I have not accepted it". The skeptic realized that all his anger, his berating of the Buddha, all the hatred and negative thoughts and the feelings that he was trying to heap on the Buddha – essentially now belong to him!! He is the owner of all those thoughts, all the anger, all the negativity. Therein lies the realization. Negative feelings, thoughts, and words towards others bring nothing but negativity to yourself. Rid your mind of them – that lightens your mind and lights it up!!

Have you wondered how unhappiness has entered our lives? For an answer, just look within. When people pick a fight without much reason, when they use bad language and spew hatred when they resort to violence, it shows how unhappy they must be – for within them lies all this hatred, jealousy, and anger. All thin negativity causes both physical and mental health problems for them and to others. My personal approach is that to be happy outside, one needs to be happy within. Our negative thoughts hurt us to no end. They create a huge barrier for happiness to come into our lives. Negativity robs of our innate nature to be happy. So, the very first and necessary requirement to be happy is to re-engineer your mind to get rid of negative thoughts, negative feelings, negative judgments, and negative actions and to become happy within.

Next, I want to distinguish between happiness and feelings of pleasure and pain. Happiness is a long-term condition of the mind whereas pleasure and pain are fleeting feelings that do not sustain. In life one passes through pain and pleasure all the time. In my 94 years of life, I have experienced many ups and downs, more downs than up!! At a young age, before I was 14 years old, I went through a lot of pain. This created a lot of negativity within me – feelings of inadequacy, anger, jealousy, hatred. At that young age, I did not process the extraordinary calmness and tolerance that my mother displayed very well. Instead, I became rebellious and vengeful.

Lacking even the basic necessities of life, living with seven others in one small dingy windowless room infested with bugs that served as the kitchen, living room, and bedroom, suffering, and pain were my constant companions. Even in the bathroom that we shared with my uncle's family, they always had priority over us. We were poor, unsure of our next meal, and always on the receiving end. We were hemmed in by constraints from all directions, in all dimensions. For a long time, we mutely accepted and kept our mouths shut. All my younger siblings too kept mum for fear of the wrathful eruptions of my grandmother. We loved our mom and we felt very deep pain at the suffering that she was going through. In contrast, she did not, at least outwardly, seem to mind all the suffering at all. She would repeatedly tell us that better days were ahead, and the present problems were simply a test our mettle. As small children, we acquiesced with our Mom. As I grew up a little, the unfairness of it all was too much to bear.

Slowly at first and more brazenly afterwards, I began hitting back at our tormentors. All the patience and forbearance that I had learned were washed away, giving place to anger and hatred! My attitude was tit for tat, revenge for revenge. I became irritable and started losing temper at the slightest provocation. This attitude of anger and dissent, of rebellion and revenge, stayed with me for a while. I disregarded my mom's appeal to calm down and be patient first and later, after I got married, my wife`s appeal as well. I got married at the age of 31 when I was a hot-headed excitable young man with a very short temper. As providence had ordained, my wife was the opposite of me. She was cool, almost never ever got excited, and never ever reacted without thinking. God knows that she tried heaven and earth to reform me!! Her calmness and reasoning would only fire up my anger even more. In fits of anger, I would utter harsh words instead of appreciating her and correcting myself. I would utter harsh hitting words with no justification. Although I moderated over time, unfortunately, such lapses lasted till my 80th year. Even though I was outwardly very harsh, I really loved and admired my wife. She was a highly cultured and good-hearted person and was probably one in a million who could tolerate this behavior from me and still take care of me. However, she was rarely in good health and would fall sick frequently. I always took good care of her when she was sick and tried my best to give her love and comfort. In my 80th year, she died of cancer after uncontrolled pain and suffering. It was finally the misery that I felt at her loss and the unbearable shock and grief that I experienced at that time that triggered my inward look, introspection, and reformation.

I realized that the 49 and half years of married life with her was indeed a time of bliss due to her goodness. I had to get over my grief and shock first. I convinced myself that it was Lord's wish to relieve her of her suffering and grant her everlasting peace. With her departure came a sense of self-realization. I felt a deep sense of guilt within me for hurting her sentiments. All I could do was to silently beg her pardon. In her life, and now in her death, she had inspired me to transform my life and improve myself. She had finally succeeded in inspiring me to start a new life, filled with positivity, gratefulness, and vigor. After all these years, I finally started a journey towards greater love, renewed compassion, and ultimately towards greater happiness.

My transformation started with the realization of what can be achieved and a quiet, guiltless acceptance of the erroneous path that I had taken until my 80th year. It is never late to transform, to reform, and to start the process of re-engineering. It is far better to do that than to continue in the same erroneous path!! Now when I get up, I feel gratitude to the Lord for granting me one more day in this wonderful world. Positive thoughts allow me now to look on the bright side of the world and of all the others that I come across. I look out and say to myself 'What a nice Day'. It matters little if it is raining, cloudy, hot, or humid. Every day is a window of opportunity to help others and help myself get better. I walk around the house seeing the pictures on the wall, of all my family including that of my wife and parents, and parents-in-and law. Likewise, I look at the pictures of our deities, and great persons like Mother Teresa, that inspire me to strive to improve myself over the course of the day. I touch the feet in the pictures of my departed elders and seek their blessings. I pray to the Lord and recite hymns seeking him to bless the whole world with peace and prosperity. Inside the cover of my prayer book, I have kept pictures of my near and dear ones. I remember each one of them and offer my heartfelt love. After that, I read the day's page of the DAILY THOUGHTS AND PRAYER published by the Ramakrishna Mission over a hundred years ago. The spiritual messages contained therein are like pearls of wisdom. I then turn to the "Friendship" book that provides good advice about positive living. Finally, I go through the daily messages on positive reflections received through email from Brahma Kumari's every morning except Sundays. I conclude these readings by reciting prayers in praise of the Lord. I do this every day and it takes not more than 30 minutes.

This daily routine every morning puts me in a positive framework for the whole day and makes me happy. I then wish my caretaker, driver, milkman, and the newspaperman. These simple acts make them smile and bring some cheer to both them and me. Without fail, I also thank my adopted sister Naomi (my neighbor) for having come into my life and the love, affection, and care she showers on me! After the demise of my wife, she has become ever more caring and watches over me like a baby!! I am so grateful for such kindness and affection!! Whenever I have the slightest health problem, she comes literally running to see me and does not leave until she had done all she could, to help me.

Our actions and reactions often build on each other and push us into situations where we feel miserable. I recall a friend asking for a loan from me once, assuring that he would pay it back in a short time. We met often after I gave him the loan amount, but he never talked about the loan. Two years went by. One day I politely asked him as to when I could expect the money back. Suddenly his facial expression changed, and he left without a word, in anger. Within two days he came and dumped the money on my table, and abruptly left. For over a year he never contacted me even once and treated me as if I was the guilty person!!! After that, I never felt like getting in touch as he had hurt my feelings badly. That friendship was lost forever. I think that if such a situation had cropped up now, I would act very differently. If I felt that he truly needed the money, I would give him the amount with no expectation of return. If I felt that he did not need the money, I would have expressed my inability to give him the loan because of his financial situation. The reactions would have been different and perhaps, the friendship would have continued. Both of us would be in a better state of understanding and happiness than we ended up now. On the other hand, I did the right thing when my brother passed away at the age of 49 years suddenly without any bank balance or savings for his wife and his two young daughters. No one came forward to assist. I have seen that many times, at a time when a person needs real help, his or her friends and family forsake the person. The love I had for my brother and the condition of his wife and daughters so moved me that I heard a call from within to rise above pettiness and offer to look after them. I understand and truly appreciate the joy with which my wife received them and looked after them for more than fifteen years. His daughters grew up with us and became our daughters. They are now well settled and extremely happy. Even more so, my wife and I were truly happy that we did what we could. Actions taken out of love and compassion beget reactions of gratitude and together, make all of us happy. In contrast, actions taken in pettiness and anger beget more anger and pettiness and make us all unhappy. I can truly say now that love and compassion are the basic guides for happy living.

Another factor that causes much disappointment and unhappiness is our expectation from others. In any relationship, even with the closest people like children or spouse, it is important to keep expectations at a minimal level. The problem with expectation in a close relationship is that it keeps increasing until it spirals and finally reaches a breaking point. I have seen this happen to several very nice people. Once I thought about this unemotionally and calmly, I realized how expectations spiral out of control. The more the other party fulfills your expectation, the higher the expectation becomes for the next time. Ultimately when expectations are not fulfilled, it leads to the souring of the relationship, disappointment, and sometimes, a sense of abandonment. Moreover, as one keeps increasing expectations, the others might want to oblige at first, but it becomes more and more onerous and burdensome for them. This combination of increasing expectations and decreasing willingness on the part of your relative or friend is almost certainly a recipe for disaster.

I have learnt to consciously keep my expectations in check with anyone, including my children. I never expect anything from anyone at any time. I have trained myself to be ready to help at any point but without expecting help or gratitude from them. I do not even expect love from family members and close friends. If they offer gratitude for something, I view it as their kindness. I immediately express my appreciation when they do so. As I practice this, I have realized that my relationships improved, and I have derived a lot of joy and happiness from these relationships. Even so, I am very conscious of not increasing my expectation in any of the relationships with my family and friends. I have consciously practiced behaving in such a congenial way, see the positives in others, and love them as much as I could. Love begets love and indifference begets indifference!! I also note that a few high-quality, positive, and love-based relationships, with no judgment, jealousy, and expectations, are all that one needs to be happy. I have also learnt to associate with a limited number of relatives and friends more intensely rather than seeking out many relationships.

Although transforming the thoughts in your mind is very valuable in living a happy life, thoughts alone are not sufficient. I firmly believe that thoughts need to be reflected in actions. A big lesson that I have learnt time and again is that if you want to do something good, you should go ahead and do it, without bothering too much about critics who might find faults. There is no such thing as a "doner's remorse"!! When you give for a good cause, your intention is more important for you than the possibilities that there could be something amiss or manipulated.

The most important takeaway from all this is that becoming happy is a conscious choice to engage in introspection, invest in thoughts that remove obstacles in the path of happiness, and undertake actions that reflect positive thoughts. *In a nutshell, I am happy always because I do not want it any other way.* It is a conscious effort because it is seldom a smooth ride. Not at all! In life, we all face problems, small or big. When we get the good news, we feel happy for a short time but immediately afterwards, we revert to our original state! At other times, we get bad news and we feel disappointed and sad but try to forget it and move on. Often, we are tormented by grief arising from sickness or death in the family or among close relatives or friends. We suffer from grief, but the natural response is to try to forget it. In all these cases, our natural response to escaping from bad news does not really result in happiness. We feel regret often and the thoughts of what we could have done differently come to us naturally. We re-live those moments of sadness and despair and suffer repeatedly. For attaining happiness, it is necessary to get out of this endless cycle but how?

My answer to this question is to focus on actions and empathy rather than keeping the thoughts internally and trying to escape from them. If you feel sad about someone, close or otherwise, think about what you could do to alleviate their suffering. How can I help heal the situation? What resources can I bring in or mobilize to address the issue? Sometimes, you may need to spend time with the sick. Sometimes, they may need financial help and you might be in a position to provide that. I believe that we should unhesitatingly stretch out and do the best to relieve the situation. This prospective active planning rather than retrospective and passive reaction can provide a path to happiness. Take the example of my brother's death that I have alluded to before. Although the grief was very real and palpable at that time, the action of supporting his family provided rich dividends in terms of satisfaction and happiness. Take the case of Nagu when her husband left her, and she was forced to fend for her young children with no means whatsoever. If my wife and I had just felt bad and turned away from helping her, it would not have produced any positive outcome or given us joy. Offering complete family support to her at her time of need has made all the difference. Now, I have someone who cares for me and looks after me like a daughter!! The more I think about what has made me happy in life, the more I realize that the positive and purposeful actions that we have initiated to relieve others' suffering are the ones that have ultimately provided happiness. I emphasize again that this is not the typical natural response. This kind of response needs to be cultivated with conscious effort.

I compliment the focus on conscious actions with mind-calming habits of meditation a few times a day and before retiring at night. I am a lot more draws to inward thinking than before. I also think back every night on whether my behavior had been right, or whether I had a negative thought. This continuous self-feedback helps me in correcting myself. By doing this daily regularly, I have made it a habit. I seem to be progressing in the right direction and hopefully, it culminates in my retaining only pure positive thoughts towards all. I liken this self-feedback process to a long-distance runner pausing to catch his breath so that he could continue to run longer and better. Meditation helps us in the concentration of the mind resulting in better willpower. It helps in overcoming bad situations.

I realize that often, it is destiny that decides what happens and no amount of worrying is going to change that. I recall that during my assignment in London, I was responsible to procure various types of hardware required by the armed forces in India. I thought that this operation was going on smoothly. Out from the blue, I got an intimation that my name has been sent to the Public Accounts Committee of the Central Government. The accusation was that I had not taken action to cancel some orders that were considered not needed by the government. This came as an unexpected shock to me. When I carried out detailed checks in my office, I found, to my surprise, several unanswered letters from the government with my chief clerk. He had no answer but to say sorry!! I did not have a credible defense and it was possible that the government would not exonerate me. I worried about it to no end and went into a deep depression. I had nightmares that this could bar my promotion and that I would be sent back to India to face charges. When this matter was brought up before the Public Accounts Committee, their financial advisor (who had worked with us in London and knew me well) brought to the notice of the chairman of the committee all the good work I had done getting millions of pounds of orders canceled with my rapport with the supplying agencies oof the French Government. After the hearing, the chairman was fully satisfied with my work and I was later told that he commented that I need to be complimented instead!! Heaving a sigh of relief, I thanked everyone for such a miracle! What else could it have been? A gentleman who had worked with me and was convinced about my uprightness in London came to my rescue while he was with the Public Accounts Committee in Delhi!! This experience convinced me that good acts never go waste. The good "sanskars" lifted me out of the depth to which I had descended!!

    Another instance that I recall is that during my tenure of over 4 years in London, I had, with prior permission, enrolled for a three-year course at the EALING Technical College. This course was to finish in June 1967. Around April 1967, I received a transfer order asking me to return to India. The authorities wanted me to leave the following month. This would have meant that my three years going to College in the evenings would go waste. Not knowing what to do, I spoke with my superior officer. He tried his best to retain me for a few more months but did not succeed. My successor was all set to report on time! I then requested for grant of two months' leave to appear for the final examinations. I had the support of my superior officer and finally, I was granted leave without pay. I would not get my salary, house rent, and heating allowances for those two months. We had not saved any money to cover this unexpected development. The landlord of my house, a serving air force officer of the Royal Air Force came just at this time from Singapore on vacation. When they came to see me, I spoke to them about my predicament. Without hesitation, they (he and his wife) agreed to waive the rent for those two months!! I am ever grateful for this act of extreme kindness that I had never expected. The landlord was a British citizen and I was really moved by his trust of a foreign official in his country!! When the time came for me to move, he even allowed me to just close the door and leave for India with no check of the inventory. I can only think that Providence had intervened on my behalf in the form of this kind man!! Finally, I was able to complete the Course and get my Post Graduate Diploma in Management Studies from the authorities!!!!

I love to end this chapter on HAPPINESS thus. When I get up, I thank the Lord for giving me one more day; I end this day as though it is my last! And go all out to make it the happiest and rewarding one.

CHAPTER 26

THE PANDEMIC OF OUR TIMES: CORONA VIRUS—COVID 19

As was the case with most people, I never knew of this till it struck us badly. The pandemic has unfortunately spread the world and has not abated in any significant way. From news reports, this nasty virus has spread to more than 212 countries around the globe resulting in millions of cases with a large number of fatalities. As of now, over five million victims have fallen prey globally. The newscasts so far indicate that it started in China, in the city of Wuhan with a population of 11 million as early as January 2020. I was blissfully unaware of the virus and its reach till March. I flew to Bombay on February 26th to celebrate my 94th birthday the next day with my children.

As of September 14, 2020, in India alone, there have been more than 4.75 million cases that are increasing at the rate of about 90,000 per day. About 2.8 million people have recovered leaving more than 86000 fatalities. Worldwide, the number of cases is a staggering 31 million with 958,000 fatalities. The magnitude of its impact on the health of people and economies is unprecedented. Moreover, there is much uncertainty about whether and how it will end. Different governments have responded differently to the virus but overall, the virus has had the upper hand. In India, we were under a strict lock-down for over 40 days in the beginning but there were too many problems to sustain such a lock-down. With lockdown, all shops were closed, train, and the bus and air services stopped plying. Most of the office staff changed the mode of working from in-person, at-the-workplace to in-home online. The whole country had the empty look of a ghost town. Work at factories declined substantially, resulting in both a loss of output and the employees losing their jobs. Most of the airways were unable to pay salaries and have warned their staff to look for jobs outside. As such, the economy of India has been one of the hardest hit with a drop of nearly 25% drop year-on-year for the first quarter of 2021 (April 1, 2020, through June 30, 2020). Governments all over the world are in a dilemma. While most value human lives over the abstract numbers of economic decline, the economic decline also includes many people who have lost their livelihoods, some who have become destitute, and many who have become non-productive. Opening up risks the possibility of an even greater resurgence of the virus whereas shutting down risks the denial of livelihood to many people with the accompanying threats of starvation, malnutrition, and mental depression. As a stop-gap measure, the Indian government remitted some money by direct transfer, but it looks like a drop in the bucket!! Top economists have urged the government to act quickly.

The economic fallout from the pandemic has been enormous in terms of human suffering. Several countries are on the verge of economic collapse. Unlike the rich countries such as the U.S., many poorer countries are highly limited in their financial and other resources to sustain such economic shocks for any length of time. The loss of jobs has hit the daily wage earners and their dependents especially hard. Many are on the brink of starvation. Children are suffering from severe malnutrition and lack of schooling. After all, most children in countries like India cannot afford two square meals a day, let alone computers and internet connections!! I go back to my days as a child who grew up in poverty and my heart goes out to all of them whose suffering is beyond description.

The pandemic has affected the seniors even more seriously than others. Seniors over 65 years of age have been advised to not venture out. At the age of 94, I am in a very high-risk category. I have strictly followed the rules recommended by health authorities such as social distancing, wearing a face mask, and not venturing out unless essential. People ask me if I am scared or worried, and how I manage my life in these times. Worrying about something that I cannot control can only exacerbate the problem! The pandemic has made me focus inwards, even more, to seek peace and tranquility. I am not afraid, but overcoming fear is not a sufficient response. All of us need to get engaged in keeping ourselves safe and healthy. I do more meditations, listen to classical music, walk inside and on the balcony of my flat, keeping a distance from others. I have reduced talking to the very minimum. Each one of us has a group responsibility – to look out for each other - and do whatever is needed to fight the pandemic. In this spirit, I keep myself updated on the pandemic's spread and the changing guidelines and follow the guidelines strictly to protect myself and others. I also try to share the guidelines with others that I am in contact with so that there is a greater awareness of how to deal with the pandemic. The important thing for me is to focus my energy on actions rather than worrying about something that I cannot control.

That said, while I am cared for and looked after, many other seniors depend on external services and other family members, to look after their daily needs. Many are in a situation where their children cannot even visit them – even when they are not well. Several older people at the lower economic strata have been devastated!! I can understand that they do not have many options.

Interestingly, the scenario in China is different. They have reported that all their patients have fully recovered. Markets have fully opened, air services restored!! The country which first became the victim appears to have become normal. The situation in most of the other parts of the world continues to be gloomy. The only way that there could be a let-up in the pandemic is if every person follows strict rules of social distancing, washing hands with soap and water, and staying indoors unless it is essential to venture outside. If every individual observes a strict regimen, then this will bring about a positive change all over the world. This requires a very high degree of group responsibility. Over many years, with the emphasis on individual liberty and self-interest doctrines, the populations world-over have moved away from the idea of group responsibility. Therefore, the idea of everyone following the rules to keep others safe is unlikely to be followed. This is particularly evident in western countries, where the opposition to lockdown is strong and there is a clamor for opening up not just the productive parts of the economy but also the restaurants, bars, beaches, etc. Beaches are back with people swimming or surfing, ignoring social distancing. While I do not have policy prescriptions, it seems prudent to balance the imperative for opening up the productive parts of the economy with the health and safety of all people, both working and non-working.

The only thing in our power as citizens is to continuously pray for everyone's welfare. Several countries are devoting considerable effort and resources to find both cures and vaccines for COVID. Vaccines developed by AstraZeneca and Oxford University, the U.S. company Moderna and China and Russia are under different stages of trials. Governments and others are signing contracts for the manufacturing and distribution of the vaccines as soon as they succeed in the trials. Hopefully, we will have effective vaccines without many side effects that could make the people less skeptical about the vaccines and which can be distributed throughout the world populations fast. Let us hope and pray that this happens soonest. The World Health Organization is urging everyone to bear in mind the need to provide vaccinations and cures to the poorer countries and save lives all the world over. I hope that effective vaccines are discovered and distributed soon enough to slow down and ultimately halt the pandemic.

While there are regulatory and other actions to be taken by governments, my focus is on my thoughts and actions in response to the pandemic. As I have written earlier, I chose to live all by myself after my wife departed. I was then just a few months short of 80 years. If I continued to live all by myself at the age of 94 during the pandemic, the risks would be too high. I would have had to interact with people to provide me the daily requirement of groceries such as fruits and vegetables. In the present context, it would have been unwise and unsafe to have even a few friends and relatives to come and see me. If I fell sick, it would be difficult for my children to care for me. All these problems of independent living would create a situation with tension and anxiety. The important thing to remember is to be flexible and respond to life changes when the environment changes.

As luck would have it, I left for Bombay on February 26th to be with my son and daughter-in-law in Mumbai to celebrate my 94th birthday. I was scheduled to return on March 3rd but when I got the first news of the virus, I decided to give it some time and I decided to go later, preferably accompanied by my son. As such, the pandemic started increasing and the plan of going back after two months was also put on hold. With no air or train services, I am blessed to have been comfortably living under the loving care of my son and his wife. I canceled my plan of traveling to the United States this year. In my own case, I need to balance the need for independent living with the possibility that it would create more problems for me and my loved ones. I have chosen to be flexible and stay with my son or in my own place when needed. This way, I could reduce and lessen potential future problems, anxieties, tensions, and worries of everyone.

I also want to express my sincere gratitude to the doctors, nurses, and other health care providers. There are reports that many of these providers themselves getting this infection and dying too. It is very unfortunate indeed and the professionals risking their lives to save others is very much akin to the armed forces who are ready to sacrifice their own life for saving the country and its people. No amount of gratitude to the front-line workers is enough in a situation like this. My younger son and his wife are both doctors in Delaware in the U.S. and are very busy, attending their clinics every day seeing patients from morning till evening. They keep telling me that at these crucial times it is their primary duty to care for the sick even at personal risk. They also continue to serve hot meals every Sunday to the needy, a charitable endeavor that they have been scrupulously doing for nearly a decade. It is at times like the nobility of the health profession and the idea of group responsibility in charity gets highlighted. As an ex-officer of the army, I have seen action on the front line number of times. Once again, I remember my wife who would be anxious and scared when I was posted to be in the frontlines. Of course, it was my duty to be there for others and my wife used to silently pray for me and my fellow officers. She would also pray for an end to these disputes. I see much parallel now with the COVID response by health officers. They are in the front line and we all pray for them. We also hope that this pandemic would come to an end and spare them this ordeal and us, our anxieties.

Positive Effects of Corona Virus

Even when the virus is ravaging the populations world-wide, and taking many lives, some small positive long-term effects would result in saving millions of lives in the future. First, the entire population of the world has been made aware of health hazards. This has increased the attention paid to health at every level – from the individual to organizations, institutions, and government. Almost certainly, this pandemic will increase the preparedness of the world to future threats from the virus. It has also exposed the security threats from sources other than armed conflicts in general. Cyber threats, threats from climate change, and other natural phenomena are being recognized more seriously after this pandemic. More immediately, there has been an emphasis on hygiene and cleanliness at the individual and local community levels. The environment has become cleaner and has thereby reduced the number of respiratory health problems. The lockdowns and quarantines in several countries have resulted in fewer planes, trains, buses, and cars polluting the atmosphere. The pollution, which was at a dangerous level before the pandemic, has come down. The sky is clear. There are less noise, less dust, and less smoke. Even in Mumbai, we can hear the birds chirping!! Handwashing with soap and water has become a habit for many, including children. In India, social distancing and greeting with folded hands – Namasthe- has become more common than shaking hands. Several employees are now working from home eliminating bus or car commuting and are learning ways of working productively from home. This could result in a reduction of carbon emissions, contributing to cleaner air to breathe. The reduction over a year has been assessed at 300 million tons. To some extent, it has improved the work/life balance for many.

In the city of Venice where one has to go from place to place in boats only, it has been reported that water has become clearer and one could see the fish in it! In China, coal consumption has dropped by 30%. I hope that a lot of these lessons learned during this pandemic will help humanity in the future to sustain this planet and lead healthier and fuller lives.

CHAPTER 27

SILENCE

My reason for delving into this subject is two-fold. The first one covers the period up to the time I came to know and realized the significance and importance of this word. The second one is to describe my experiments and the realization of its meaning and importance.

The word "silence" had almost no impact in my day to day dealings till I was 80 years old. I seldom heard of anyone talking about it, perhaps because I did not even realize that it was something that one should study. Like most others, my first experience with this word was in grade school where our teachers repeatedly admonished us to maintain silence. After that, I understood silence in the context of listening to something – for example, whenever I attended a lecture, we had to switch off or put our phones in silent mode, or when I attended a music concert, the rules and norms required us to switch off our phones and maintain silence so that we (and others) could listen to the music in peace. Even in our practice of yoga asanas, the emphasis was on making the body supple and strong, not on silence. Suffice it to say that I was ignorant about the power and importance of silence until I was around 80 years old.

It all changed for me when I went for a vacation to Hong Kong via Bangkok in the year 2006/2007. On the flight, I sat next to an elderly Australian lady and started chatting with her. During our interaction, she asked me if I had undergone a Vipassana Course. I felt a little embarrassed that as an Indian, I had not heard of it. I had to learn about it from a non-Indian! She gave me a bird's eye view of a ten-day Vipassana course packed with many hours of meditation classes. When I returned to Bangalore, I registered for the course. It was run on the Buddhist model. At the risk of repeating some of the things that I have talked about elsewhere in the book, I will give a short description of the course here.

The meditation classes start daily at 4:30 am and goes on till about 9:30 pm with breaks for breakfast, shower, lunch, and dinner. The students were drawn from all walks of life the world over. The main emphasis throughout the course was on concentration and how to learn to be silent. The course is run free of lodging and boarding charges. The organizers were doing this as a charitable endeavor to inculcate the habit of observing silence. On reporting, we registered and handed over our wallet, cell phone, and other items we had brought with us, for safekeeping until the completion of the course.

On the first day, we assembled in the evening for a briefing. The chief instructor welcomed us and spoke sweetly about the potential benefits that we could get during the ten-day course. He emphasized that the going would be tough but exhorted us to be patient and to bear the ups and downs so that we could get used to observing silence. He assured us that true silence is extremely beneficial to our mental balance and happiness. Even though the first few days would be tough, we were told to bear it so that we could reap the future advantage. I was not used to getting up so early and sit still for hours and hours passively!! We were advised to have the moral strength not to yield to the physical dictates. In my case, I suspected that living alone, and getting up so early would mean a long day. I started wondering how I could endure ten days of silence and passivity. I love reading or listening to music for hours after dinner and then go to bed in a happy mood. How could I spend the whole day in silence and then go to bed without music?

On the first day, we assembled at the Buddha Meditation Hall. As instructed, I sat with my eyes closed, trying to concentrate on my breathing. I tried but now and then would adjust the sitting posture. When you see everyone else sitting still motionless, you get the motivation to do the same. The first session of 90 minutes passes off quite easily, perhaps because of the novelty of it. After a while, my back started hurting and I felt exhausted. For the first time in our lives, we were going through this experience purely to benefit our minds. Even after the first session, I was feeling uncertain about completing the course. I overcame my self-doubt by assuring myself that the ultimate gains come only after initial pain – that seems to be the way of nature. After the first session, we were served a hot breakfast and delicious tea. Buddhist music was played during the meditation. This music was so inspiring that it kept me going during the meditation classes in the afternoon. While meditating I stealthily opened my eyes and saw a few of the others standing or sitting with legs stretched as they must have felt uneasy.

On the second day, two students left, perhaps because they could not bear this routine. The first two days were focused on concentrating on the natural rhythm of breathing. From day 3 onwards, the meditation was altered to concentrate on different parts of the body starting with the right eye, then the left eye, and finally the whole face. After this was completed, we were asked to observe the right shoulder followed by the left one ending up with both the shoulders. I was amazed at the inward transformation that I experienced!! Just by concentrating on a part of the body, I could feel some heat in that part. I had the same feeling with the top of my head. It was almost like a hot furnace!! I could not believe that just the concentration of the mind could have this kind of result. Each day was spent focusing on different parts of the body, separately at the beginning and then together at the end. The whole experience created an indescribable peaceful and refreshing feeling. As the program advanced, so did my ability to concentrate. This gave me a divine feeling within. Finally, I reached a stage when I could sharpen my meditation to feel a bright spiritual light! I do not have words to describe this miraculous change. I realized that I could concentrate so well because of the absolute silence around me and the power of concentration could energize me so much. While sitting silently, we watch the world passing around us. I could listen to silence and learn from it. Silence is all-powerful and, in a way, silence can make a point much more powerfully than the loudest affirmation of it.

I have since studied the sayings of eminent yogis on the subject of silence. Paramahamsa Yogananda, one of the most impactful yogis to travel to the U.S. and establish the practice of yoga there, says that there are thoughts in the Temple of Silence that is too great for our hearts to speak. I certainly needed this experience. I have always been a very talkative person from birth for almost 80 years. I realized that I had nearly lost the ability to listen to others. I would cut them off with my verbal diatribes. Regretfully, I did not even listen to my own wife. Although it is late, I finally realized the power of silence, the beauty of listening, and the serenity that comes with it. I have personally experienced while sitting in the silence of deep meditation, bubbles of joy raising with no outside interference. This takes one towards the Divine (taken from one of the quotes that I read).

Many decades ago, I had done a yoga course of 10 days under the guidance of Swamy Sivananda who had established his Aashram called the Divine Life Society in Haridwar. This Society was located at a very scenic spot and to reach it, we had to walk over the Lakshman Jhoola (hanging bridge) over the River Jhelum. Swamiji was a doctor who had turned into a sage. Before attending the course, I read available material on Swamiji's method of meditation. He advocated concentrating on a diety or any symbol. One had to sit erect with legs crossed with hands resting on the thighs. I practiced it and a feeling of inner happiness arose within, freeing me from the outside world. I continued this method for some time. The yoga classes that I attended were conducted at Adipur, Kutch, Gujarat. Yet, in all the ten days, the word "Silence" was never uttered once!!

To me, Vipassana was the true starting point in my meditational search. After successful completion, I started meditating twice a day for an hour each. I had earmarked times for doing this. I was disciplined and regular in my meditation practice and continued this without break for several months. I have the habit of looking out for new learning experiences. I don't get satisfaction from a daily routine if it does not lead to further learning.

My quest to learn more and more brought me closer to the teachings of Ramakrishna Paramahamsa. The Ramakrishna Mission was a few kilometers from my residence. I started visiting this center and meditating in their big Hall. A big marble statue of Ramakrishna was placed there on a pedestal. The statue of Sharda Devi was kept in the adjoining room. I used to spend around an hour concentrating on Paramahamsa while remaining still. The huge hall had scores of meditators maintaining pin-drop silence. Some of the Swamijis were also seen meditating without a semblance of movement. They would sit for longer periods than I could, but I tried my best. This was also a very rewarding experience.

After a few months, I suddenly noticed the Brahmakumari Ashram just a street away. I had never applied my mind as I was not aware of their details. My thirst for more forms of meditation led me to the Brahma Kumari Ashram. I was welcomed with much affection and hospitality. I learnt it was started in 1930 in Hyderabad, Sindh Province now part of Pakistan, and has branches all over the world. It was headed by Shiv Baba, a jeweler who gave up his lucrative business to start this Mission. People venerate him as the human incarnation of Lord Shiva. It is now managed and runs efficiently by the Brahma Kumaris. They are committed to selfless service. The entrance is free. The Ashram is housed in a three-storied massive structure. I underwent a seven-day orientation course with them. After that, I started attending their meditation sessions. Here one concentrates on Shiv Baba. I continued this form of meditation – called Raja Yoga - for some time.

Now I was armed with various ways of meditating, I realized that the central theme of all meditation is more or less the same. There is a strong emphasis on remaining silent for long hours while concentrating on something. The differences are superficial and only a matter of taste. I mostly stuck to the Vipassana way. I have found thousands of videos on YouTube on meditation varying from short to long duration. I can now watch it on my television in the comfort of my room. I have continued this daily practice every day. These videos are set in beautiful natural locations and accompanied by soul-stirring music.

I want to end this chapter by emphasizing the significance of this word SILENCE. I have derived abundant benefits by just observing silence. This has changed me deeply, making me patient and peaceful. I listen to others a lot more than before. With silence, I enjoy others' talks. To quote Mahatma Gandhi, the seeker of truth has to be silent and listen to the still small voice that is always speaking within us. If we speak, then we miss the voice of our inner conscience. Silence is a part of the spiritual discipline that ultimately draws you towards truth. Silence helps you surmount your own weaknesses such as the proclivity to exaggerate, the urge to suppress or modify the truth, and pretend to be what you are not – just to receive recognition from others. A man of few words is rarely thoughtless in his speech. He will measure every word. Many of us are impatient to listen but talk, thinking that the others would listen!! It is really a weakness, not a strength.

EPILOGUE

This is my second book. The first one was titled 'MARATHON AT 90. It was published after my 91st birthday in 2017. The present one is SEEKING HAPPINESS---MY JOURNEY---REENERGIZING MY MIND. I have gone deep into my life's journey over the last 94 years that transformed me from an unhappy to an ever-happy person with a zest for life. I grew up in poverty and misery and the anger at the unfairness of it all was deeply instilled in my mind for a long time. I was unhappy during my earlier years because of all the pent-up anger within me and were wasted in cursing, fault-finding, and intolerance. I was determined to get over the pitiable condition of my younger years and made up my mind to pursue to achieve my goal. I could not think of college education when we found paying school fees even problematic. There were offers of financial assistance, but these were conditional to my agreeing to marry their daughter at the end. I preferred to be a metric. At age 17, I traveled over 1600 miles in search of an opening. I was weak and looked as if I was only 10 years old and no employer was willing to offer a job. They wanted to me study. With immense determination and a lot of luck, I managed to get an entry to the Indian Military Academy. With this milestone, I had the opportunity to improve my prospects. I could become financially self-sufficient and help my parents with the education of my siblings. Slowly, I changed in some ways. With the help of my wife, I brought up my sister-in-law and her two daughters, educated them, got them married, and helped settle them down. They are all living a comfortable life. We also helped many to stay with us and acted as their guardians during their college studies at nearby stations. My army career went well for over 31 years, but I decided to quit as I found the atmosphere getting vitiated day by day. I worked thereafter in a civilian capacity for 17 years until I was 67.

I was blessed to have an understanding wife who bore all this without getting worked up herself. She continuously tried to guide me into a path of happiness, but I did not know it at that time. However, my total love for her protected us. Although she was mentally strong and her mind was always tranquil, she was weak in her body and fell sick very often. Both my sense of duty and my love for her gave me the incentive and the energy to take the best care of her. Her death in 2005 was a catastrophic loss for me. My true reformation started in earnest only after her demise. I felt the need to change my life for the better. I had to get over the shock first and all the negativity after that. I finally calmed down and with reflection and introspection, found a path towards reformation.

First, I decided to live independently in my flat while keeping the best possible relationships with my children and grandchildren. My children were keen to keep and look after me, but I could see that over-dependence on children harms the relationship with them. Denying privacy to them and myself did not seem like the best way going forward. Instead, I was determined to learn to be independent. My second decision was to look after myself physically. I needed to exercise and be as physically fit as possible, to enable independent living. I also had to make sure that my diet and other habits promote my health. Falling sick and becoming weak were not the right options if I had to succeed in independent living. Towards this end, I made arrangements for my caretaker Nagu to take care of my household affairs such as cooking and cleaning, and my driver Lokesh to drive me around wherever I needed to go, Apart from just being physically fit, I started challenging myself both physically and mentally. I started running half marathons of 13.1 miles starting at age 84, until and including when I was 91 years of age. It helped that I was awarded the first prize in my age category four times. At the age of 89, I learnt backstroke, after taking 38 coaching classes. I continue to challenge myself physically in a realistic way, that is, to go beyond what I consider possible for me but only by a little. I challenge myself mentally every day solving puzzles, playing brain games, reading books, etc. Third, I started improving myself spiritually through meditation and breathing exercise under guidance from several meditation centers. I also began to introspect and reflect on my behavior every day to improve continuously and become a better person. I have trained myself to be positive and derive positive energy from nature while banishing negative thoughts from my mind. I have developed an attitude of gratitude to all the people who have directly or indirectly helped me. I am also grateful to the almighty for giving me this opportunity, to nature for providing me the ability to appreciate, and to my departed wife for enabling me to transform into a better human being. I have continuously tried to transcend my ego and seek forgiveness from all those whom I might have offended in the past and unknowingly now. I have personally contacted people whom I had offended before, to seek their pardon. I believe that over time, I have become a different person with more positive thoughts and habits. I realize that the journey is never complete, but I am invigorated and energized to continue on this path for as long as I live.

Finally, I am saying with humility and gratefulness that I live my life with a spirit of service. I am lucky to have such a wonderful family and a few relatives and friends who lend their hand in times of need. Life has given me more than I expected. I convey my grateful thanks to all who have played their part in making me what I am

I end this with a prayer to the Almighty to keep me this way for as long as He pleases.

I also seek the blessings of the readers of this book.

Let everyone's motto be:

THINK HAPPY STAY HAPPY AND BE HAPPY!!

APPENDIX A

INSPIRATIONAL THOUGHTS FOR FURTHER CONTEMPLATION

Inspirational Thoughts:

- ➤ Have a positive attitude towards life. Consciously develop only positive thoughts about everyone you come across in life. In particular, do not be judgmental about your family members, your friends, your colleagues, and others. Suppress negative thoughts. Be helpful but not critical in a negative way.

When you are inundated with negative news, when other people are critical about you, and you are surrounded by a negative environment, it is hard to be positive. Yet do it. It requires conscious and continuous effort. Be patient. You become the change agent to remake your environment. Amazingly, as you turn more positive, most others turn positive as well, and the environment becomes positive and conducive to happiness.

- ➤ Invest in your health and physical fitness. Diet is important. Consciously refrain from eating too much sugar, fat, and other substances that might give short term pleasure but result in long term health issues. Exercise regularly in a way that you can sustain over time and consistent with your needs.

Physical ailments and health problems could result in frustration and unhappiness. A conscious effort to improve and sustain health and fitness goes a long way in leading a happy life.

- ➤ Keep yourself busy and mentally active. An idle mind is a devil's workshop where unhappiness is brewed.

It is important to occupy yourself with activities throughout your wakeful period. These need not be momentous activities. Even household chores are fine. At the same time, consciously keep your mind challenged and active. Solve puzzles if you have to, read books and articles in your area of interest, but do something that keeps the mind active. This is particularly important for those who are retired and for those who are employed in corporations or government. For the retired, spending time gossiping or passively watching TV, etc. are recipes for long term unhappiness. For the employed, it is important to rise above the defined routine duties in the job description. Invest your time in creative and innovative ideas, whether or not they are related to your world.

- ➤ Love others. Be generous. Be helpful. The more you give, the happier you become.

Generosity towards others – giving with love in your heart – brings more happiness than you think. Consciously try to love others beyond yourself and your family. Empathize with others in need – both financial and psychological. If possible, get engaged in charitable work. Always help those in need – whether or not they ask for it.

- Introspect and try to define a purpose in life – make life more meaningful to you

Think not merely of what you have done in life – think of what you can do. There are always things that you can do to help others and thereby help yourself. Do not let the current circumstances and context define you. Try to define the circumstances and context where you want to be. Having a purpose in life provides and sustains motivation and could inspire you. Happiness comes as a byproduct of meaningfulness in life.

- Try to be independent in life. Do not choose the easy path of depending on family and friends to do things for you that you can do or manage yourselves. If you need help on a continuous basis, employ someone outside the family to do that for you – and treat that person as part of the family

Continued dependence on family and friends leaves both you and them unhappy. By all means, be close to them, engage with them, and enjoy their company – but living with them as a dependent is fraught with problems. Unless you don't have any other reasonable option, be independent.

- Expect less from others. Offer more.

Much unhappiness results from unrealistic expectations, particularly from family members and close relatives. It is critical to hold back the impulse to expect more and more from those who initially fulfill the expectations. Ultimately, cascading expectations lead to disappointment and destroys happiness. Independent living helps limit the expectations of you from others. While not feeding the expectations, be prepared to do more, and offer more. This leads to greater happiness.

- Focus on outcomes but do not invest in them. Invest in your effort. Happiness is not conditional

Many of us have trained ourselves to look for happiness outside of us. "If only" I have "...", then I will be happy. Say, if only I got the promotion, I would be happy – or if only I could find an understanding life partner, then I would be happy. This conditional approach to happiness is fundamentally flawed. Perhaps you have most of the things you wished for 10 years back. Did that make you happy? Conditioning your mind on any outcome is a recipe for disappointment and unhappiness. Instead, let the desired outcome just define the direction of your journey but make your journey enjoyable.

➢ Develop patience, determination, and regularity. Happiness is a process, not an event. Determination in your actions and regularity in your habits facilitate that process.

A patient investment that is regular, controlled, and non-emotional is more likely to pay off better than a shot-gun approach. Some people might be naturally engineered to be happy but most of us are not. We need to consciously and rigorously develop approaches that make our lives happy. The process could be a long one, an arduous one, and a hard one – but it is worth it. Keep at it, with determination and patience – re-engineer your life step by step.

APPENDIX B

TESTIMONIALS

Nimish Dayalu

Brigadier Kripalu is my grandfather. I have looked up to him admirably ever since I can remember. Composed disposition, friendly demeanor and humility have been a part of his repertoire. Another notable feature has been his high energy level, similar to that of a child. He uses his high energy level to weave meaningful connections. His selflessness indicates his understanding of the cosmos and our interconnection through a complex web. He is me; I am him; you are him, all of us in different vessels and yet the same. After spending time with him I have realized that we spend much time clinging on to our experiences. If it is not the past, we are often worried about what is in store for us tomorrow. What really matters is the "here and now"
MUST HAVES- Friends, family, freedom, contemplation to relieve anxiety, health, food, shelter, clothes, good sleep
COULD HAVES- Grand house, servants, material possessions, travel, fish, meat
NOT NECESSARY- Fame, power
These are the lessons I have learnt from my grandfather.

Chotu

My dear Uncle Brigadier Kripalu is an example that I often dream to follow and emulate. He is and has always been a honest achiever of immense goodness, friendship and a simple human being. A dedicated son to his parents, the most helpful to his siblings, a devoted husband, a caring father, and a loving grandfather. In his earlier book I have mentioned that he stays a beacon of strength this will always be so till I rest in peace. His life style has clarified success, happiness and pleasure . In his style of living it's not that success only brings happiness. In the same vein I must add doing your nitya karma heralds both pleasure and success. In this context he is out and out a humane person. What needs to be understood is, it is not only his family which is in focus. He is there for any person that needs his guidance. His affection is pure and there for those who are in contact with him. This book which themes on happiness is his cherished life's mantra. I have no doubt that his open style which is noble and simple will be a pathfinder for many.

Srinivas Prasad

They say that happiness cannot be pursued, it must ensue naturally. I cannot think of anyone who has a better appreciation of this than Brig Kripalu. He has mastered the ability to redefine his sense of purpose and bring meaning to life. Brig is learning something new every day. He is constantly discovering new ways of connecting with everything around him, finding new ways of expressing his love and appreciation for family and friends, pushing his physical endurance, and spreading wisdom and love through his writing. Happiness follows from who he is, what he does and the lives of the people he touches.

Jayakumar N R

Brig. Kripalu {Kumar's maternal uncle-my mother Smt. Ratna's brother) we fondly call him Gaddu Uncle, has been epitome of discipline and resilience his whole life. He is a man with extreme will power, happiness and kindness in his heart. There is a famous song in kannada "Oh, €unavar*ha, Oh, Gunamntha, Oh, Gunauantha...nlnna Gtmagana msadalu, padagcle siguthilla.{ Gunavantha – nice characture,Gunagana madalu -to describe the tharacter, padagale siguthilla – equivalent words not available. These words are very much applicable to our dearest Gaddu Uncle. We bet those who understand this say will agree with us. He is such a nice person in all respect that to describe him we are not getting any words. His one specialty is that he is loved by all aged groups, means small children aged, middle aged and senior citizens. Wherever he goes he creates a very good atmosphere around and makes the people enjoy each and every moment- He is a very kindhearted person and is ready to help whoever needs his help "He is simple yet dignified. When one look at him feel like respect him. We cannot put into words to tell about this great man. Our heart fills with happiness, love, respect, and gratitude to this lovely GADDU UNCLE. It is commendable that this great man carME up from the grass root level and rose to a fairly good position in Indian Army. He is a sole reason for many others to come up in life and became good citizens of this country. We conclude our write up by quoting a famous saying from the great scholar Shakespeare, which suits our beloved Uncle in all ways. Shakespeare said: I always feel happy. You know why? Because* I don't expect anything from anyone. Expectations always hurt. Be Happy & keep smiling. You live for yourself & before you speak, listen. Before you write, thank. Before you spend, earn. Before you pray, forgive. Before you hurt, feel. Before you hate, love. Before you quit, try. Before you die, live.

Gita Jayanth

Give, Give, Give, Give, this joy of giving is the secret of your happiness, Doddappa. Your sheer presence spreads Happiness. You are selfless, always willing to come forward to give and in the process have touched many lives. I am truly blessed to be guided by you in every step of the way. You are and will continue to be my inspiration. Keep smiling. Happiness Always!

Asha Sampath

Happiness is often considered subjective; it is one's sense of wellbeing. It is also attributable to the biochemicals serotonin, dopamine, and oxytocin. Brig. Kripalu, my 'Dodappa,' is a terrific example of someone who has mastered both the art and science of happiness. He is able to experience happiness over extended periods - is this because he is blessed with the 'right' chemical disposition or because he mastered the art of manipulating his mind? To be honest, it is a bit of both. The chemical balance is because of the effort he makes in maintaining health. However, I believe the real trick is in how he manages his mind. Dodappa's discipline and way of life have helped train his mind to look for happiness in everything. In his mind, there is no place for negative feelings; he has the rare ability to face both the pleasant and unpleasant events in his life with poise. Moreover, even at 94, he is constantly trying to reinvent himself and be the best he can be. By doing so, he remains engaged in the lives of his children, grandchildren and friends. He continues to stay happy and share happiness with whoever he interacts irrespective of their age, diversity and background. He is loved and respected by all. His positive and content nature have helped him stay relevant, for which he feels immensely blessed and truly happy. Dodappa's wonderful life reminds us all that, "Happiness begins within."

Vinod Kripalu

Daddy has exemplified what a happy life is all about...it's about a meaningful life… it's about usefulness to others… it is about never shrinking from your duties...it's about self-discipline...essentially a virtuous life. What is amazing is his constant quest and success at self-mastery. Clearly, he continues to put in the ongoing hard work necessary to achieve this. Love him like no other.

Varsha Kripalu

When I think of Brigadier Kripalu, what doesn't come to mind? He is strong, fearless, kind, compassionate, and most of all an absolute joy to be around. I don't know what I did to get to have him as my grandfather, but I will not question it. Whenever I call him on the phone and ask, "how is your day going?", he always replies "amazing! how could life get any better?" Keep in mind that he is a widower who lives alone and doesn't work during a pandemic. The world has so much to learn from this man who truly has the greatest zest for life that I have ever seen. There aren't adequate words to describe the source of inspiration that he provides for me. If I can adopt even a fraction of his outlook on life, I think I have many happy years left ahead.

Anand Kripalu

I have come across many inspirational leaders and people in my life and career who are worth emulating. But my ultimate hero is my Dad! The greatest privilege of taking a job in Bangalore 7 years ago was that I would be in the same city as him - for the first time since I was 12 years old. And the lockdowns over the last 6 months has been the privilege of a lifetime as we have largely been together - watching movies, having a drink or just being around each other. What amazes me is how busy he is at 95! Just the sheer discipline and drive. From cracking the toughest sudokus, to walking for 45-60min even with intense pain, to reading every paper or magazine, to hearing meditation music in the afternoons, to taking several calls from the family and grandchildren, to a drink in the evening and watching a serial at night. Not a moment to be wasted. If there was a walking example of living life to the fullest - this is it, literally! The endeavor and motivation to hand writes 250 pages for his second book is itself a feat. The narrative of how to be happy is a gift to all of us who are in every way far less - and is a lesson of how to see the world as 'a glass half full' and make the most of every opportunity. As he says, being happy is a state of mind. In his case it is also a state of body, just in the sheer way he takes care of himself to be fit. It's not just him being happy. He has this way of infecting happiness with whoever he comes in touch with. Whether they are family, his friends, my friends, or even my office colleagues. He has this knack to quickly become the center of attention and energy - and happiness. What else can you ask for from your father. A Dad like no other, who will come running whenever you need him. No matter what. Even today. Proud of you Daddy.

Pravas Mishra

To talk about Kripalu Uncle in a few words is not possible but I'll try. Him and Ammani aunty welcomed me into their home 25 years ago when I first came to Bangalore as a college student. The love I received was so genuine and the acceptance in their hearts complete. Kripalu uncle was and is the most charming man I ever met. Always a gentleman. So self-sufficient, wants to do everything himself. He has something good to say about everybody. That amazes me. He always finds a quality, habit, attribute in the other person, to admire and praise. He is so full of energy and lives his life to the fullest, spending long hours listening to music and solving soduku. He puts those fractions of his age to shame with his vitality and enthusiasm for life. One other habit I admire about uncle is his discipline, he walks or exercises without fail every day, and had done so forever! Last few years he even participated in various marathons. I can honestly say that to know him and aunty enriched my life. I wish him the very best for this book and pray for his continued good health. Happiness. There is no body better equipped to write about Seeking Happiness than Brig Kripalu. He carries a positive outlook in life, as he travels along this path. Happiness to me is a state of mind, where one chooses to be happy, in most situations, irrespective of conditions and people, and sometimes even in spite of it! And as we embrace life with joy and happiness, outwards and within, we soon find ourselves in bliss. As humans with conditioned minds, we need to constantly remind ourselves, but the results are multifold and positive.

Abhinav Kripalu

It is hard to describe some things in life, especially when they have such a heartfelt impact on so many. Thatha's ever-so optimistic outlook on life is one of those things. It shines light on our flawed tendencies to over-magnify trivialities and blur the bigger picture. When you think of a typical day for a ninety-year-old man, you definitely do not think of marathons, music concerts and malt. You do not think of traits like independence and exuberance. You do not think of someone who lives half the year 8000 miles away. The only word appropriate is "outlier". A true anomaly that has positively impacted society in a plethora of ways, and what we can only aspire to make the "normal." He always has a 'live and let live' attitude. It's something you don't expect from past generations. The fluidity with which he interacts with people of different ages is mesmerizing. Had I been unaware, my intuition would tell me I am conversing with a friend (a fairly adventurous one at that!). I'm extremely proud to be a part of his lineage, and I can only hope to attain a fraction of his inner fulfillment.

Sukanya Kripalu

If there was a concept of 360-degree happiness, it would be epitomized by Daddy. He lives and breathes contentment, positivity and joyousness. Whenever I have called him from Mumbai to ask how he was, I would receive one answer - 'On top of the world'. No problems. No aches and pains. No complaints whatsoever. There are many qualities he demonstrates which make him a person to emulate - his dedication towards physical fitness and exercise, his discipline and adaptability with regard to his diet, his commitment towards meditation and spirituality and even his two stiff Johnnie Walkers in the evening! Somehow, he manages to fit all this seamlessly into a regular day. But his truly outstanding quality is his positivity and ability to connect with different people across different cultures - whether it is family or our friends and colleagues, each one has a unique relationship with him. He also has the knack of straddling different age groups - from his 101-year-old aunt to his young grandchildren. He is truly a role model not only for our family, but even to people who have met him just once. That's the power of Daddy. God bless you Daddy, may we all continue to have your love and ashirwad for a long, long time to come.

Chetana Kripalu

Every time I feel down and sad, like I want to blame anybody around me for my sadness, the thought of Daddy (my father-in-law) lifts me up instantly. I always remember him telling me how he would count his blessings to get out of this funk, and how he would exercise gratitude during these times. "Every morning when I wake up I thank God that I have another wonderful day on this earth", said Daddy once when I asked him how he managed to keep himself upbeat. Gratitude is one of the best ways to keep ourselves happy; it brings a very warm and fuzzy feeling. Those words will remain with me to remind me of how I should live my life everyday like it is my last day on earth. Another life lesson that i learned from daddy is not to have expectations from anyone, not even from the people closest to you. When one has expectations and the other does not live or deliver up to those expectations it brings about emotions of anger, frustration, and hatred for that person. This is a burden too much to carry and sometimes it lasts for a lifetime. The ability to mold himself to other interests and adjust to any lifestyle life demands is a very unique quality that daddy has which enables him to be happy and excited all the time. These are only some of his wonderful virtues that have helped me to learn how to always be positive in any condition.

Meera Kripalu

There aren't enough words to even describe how incredible my grandfather is. I always knew that he was resilient and strong beyond compare, but it was really in the last few years that I realized how truly remarkable he is. His positivity despite whatever is going on in his life or in the world, whether it is a global pandemic, the death of a loved one, or an injury, is truly inspiring. Whenever I call him to ask him how his day is going or how he is feeling, he always has such a positive outlook on life, stating that he is great, and that his life could not be better. The best part about talking to him is that I know he is being completely genuine; when he says that he is doing great and that he is grateful for each day, I know he means it with every fiber of his being. Thatha exudes positivity to the highest degree, showcasing to all of us how we should strive to be. I am so grateful to have him as my role model, biggest source of inspiration, grandfather, and best friend all in one. Thatha is truly one in a billion.

Pam Eppes

What exactly is happiness? For a visual definition or example one would just need to look at you. Happiness is much more than being joyful. It is about a total state of well-being. It is about understanding that you are living a good life when you have that deep sense of contentment. You Dear Daddy epitomize this notion of well meaning. You live each day to the fullest ad you are not intimidated by what life brings you that day. You dive in and take the experience by hand and make it your own. I also think that your deep happiness comes from the fact that you live each day without expectations from others or yourself, therefore are not subjected to feelings of disappointment, failure or loss if those expectations do not come to fruition. By not having expectations you are able to invest yourself fully in life's experiences. When I see you all I see is pure joy? You find delight in the little things such as a good cup of chai as much as you do in the bigger things like completing a half marathon in your 90(s). And when one is in your company there are no other feelings except and joy. If I had to define happiness in 2 words they would be "Daddy Kripalu."

Ricky Singh

A wise man once said that to live a good life, one must always keep his fist open. The open fist symbolizes the desire to not only give away worldly possessions and knowledge, but also receive advice and knowledge. Few people have lived their lives with a more open or bigger fists than our dear "Kripalu Uncle". His life is a masterpiece in how to live your life well and for those of us who have been fortunate to have met him and interacted with him, he has been a great influence on us and he has guided us and then stepped aside to allow us to flourish. His ethic has been crystal clear from the first day, focus on the immediate without losing sight of the future. The lessons he has taught us for our lives and careers have been tremendous. Be punctual and be on time, share stories, laugh openly and as often as you can, balance your work with your personal life, take pride in whatever you do, and respect your body and nature. He is one of the most charismatic, positive and infectious personalities that I have ever had the joy of meeting. He inspires me to try and push my limits and spread positivity and goodness in this world full of negativity and meanness. I have the greatest of respect for this great personality and wish Uncle the best of health and I hope that he continues to spread the rays of joys and happiness to everyone that comes in contact with him.

Sridhar M. Reddy

Dear Nana, It's been more than 4 years you know me, such a short time you come to know me very well which shows your true gentle love and affection towards us and people and your keen interest in many lives you have preached, touched and lifted some and also have made a circle of good friends for life, as you love music, enrich peace within you and around your present, no one can take away from you. Your present at social gathering and parties where I have observed teaming of people are always followed you, admiring your enthusiasm, relentless smile which made the moment further live. I wish you the best and love always.

Anonymous

A man that defies any elderly stereotype and is truly young! He ran twice as much the distance than I do in a day, and he is thrice as old! Our conversations were truly memorable as he made me feel the care that I would receive from family and I could also have unfiltered conversations like I do with a friend. One day, in one of our many conversations about life, I'll always remember him telling me about happiness 'between a taker and giver of happiness, a giver will always be happier!' A true provider/patron (you can choose) of happiness and wisdom!

Ranga Srivatsa

I have always walked away after a meeting with Uncle Happier than before I entered...Uncle is a real pleasure to be with. Uncle's happiness begins from within. Understanding himself and his connection with a superior force. From inner to outward, his happiness stems from training his mind to make the best of the situation at all stages, overcoming odds, accomplishing self-established goals, patiently listening, sharing with humility and avoiding judgement in his people interactions. Uncle's next book should be on maintaining self-discipline! He has managed himself mentally and physically unlike few. His best practices have contributed in his ability to remain internally and externally happy. Anyone following a fraction of his drill will be a beneficiary of happiness! Uncle's happiness besides all of the above is also a reflection of his son's and their immediate family members. Their incredible success, support and encouragement is a boon that has nurtured its way into accentuating his happiness! Uncle is the posterchild model of consistently remaining happy and being contented!

Alka and Bharat Puri

Dear Uncle, you have written a book on such an interesting topic -- happiness. It's something that is very difficult to understand, as a lot of factors like money, beauty, success have nothing to do with happiness. It is also very difficult to define how to be happy. And yet, happiness is indeed very simple -- some human beings, despite of having not much/ having many challenges, are still very happy. We find you as a great example of happiness. You always seem so contented and happy, even though there must be challenges and worries you may have. So, we are both very proud to be writing this for your book, and we do hope some of your happiness rubs off on us. We would like to read your book and discover the art of happiness -- something you truly personify.

Nicole

You have shown time and time again the courage to be open to all that life has to offer. This unwavering courage has led you to a life full of meaning and purpose. You define wholehearted living. Thatha you have cultivated a life of authenticity, compassion, creativity, gratitude, and joy. I am continually inspired and in awe of your vitality and zest for life. You have taught us time and time again that each and every one of us are responsible for creating our own happiness. A few lessons you have taught us by your example is to always be satisfied with what we have, be grateful for everything, always be adaptable, be enthusiastically positive, and to be graciously generous. Thatha your open heart, eager mind, and spirited soul has led you to rise strong and dare greatly. You are a life force! I am honored to have you in my life. My prayer for you is my gratitude to you. With much love and admiration Nicole (your adopted granddaughter).

Saurav & Shefali

Happiness is a state of mind. It's a very simple and clear statement but far easier said than done. In today's day and age where we are constantly chasing the next milestone, the next promotion, we tend to get stuck in a rat race full of undue stress and getting bogged down with seemingly no end in sight – in turn making us stew in stress and unhappiness more often than not, losing sight of the big picture. This coming from two 31-year olds, who were high school sweethearts, have had all the opportunities and support from family and friends with no real obstacles in life. It's at these moments of unhappiness that we take a moment to sit down, and really think of thatha. A 94-year old gentleman, whose immense gusto for life sheds great perspective on what really matters. Saurav always says, "whenever I am feeling crazy stressed like there is no way out and get completely bogged down, I only think of thatha and his positivity, and it immediately changes my attitude & helps me focus on what is really important in life." Seeing him today, you would never imagine the tremendous hardships he has overcome in his life. It is almost impossible to understand how a man exudes so much positivity and happiness and is thankful for every day – but that really is thatha! He is the living embodiment of happiness being a state of mind, something we must all strive to learn from him. There are very few people in the world that have this outlook on life, and we are so blessed to have him as our grandfather and be some small part of the happiness that has touched the lives of numerous people around the world!

Charmaine and Naomi

Happiness is not a goal...it's a by-product of a life well-lived." That is the way Thatha has lived his life. He brings happiness and cheer as soon as he steps into a room. He has taught us to be positive always in every aspect of life. He does not allow anyone to get lonely or sad. "The best way to cheer yourself is to try to cheer someone else up." That is our Brigadier ♥♥♥

Sridevi

It is indeed a pleasure for me to write about uncle and his book. He has been like a father figure to me. I have learnt a lot about life from him and every time I interact with him, I feel I have so much more to learn from him. It is my good fortune that he visits us for a few weeks every year in Dallas. These weeks that he spends with us provide us with an opportunity to learn how to practice positive living, improve our attitudes, control our emotions, and become stress-free. His life lessons have made my life better and happier. One of the primary things I have learnt from him is his positive attitude, optimism, and passion for whatever he does. His amazing ability to look at the positive side of even situations that are challenging, has inspired me to try to do the same thing. This one thing alone has had a transforming effect on me – making me happier and less stressed and less anxious. I can now see how his optimism and his passion have resulted in his being always happy and stress-free in life. I would also mention a number of other traits that I have tried to follow. He is always very kind-hearted and tries to help people around him. I have seen how empathetic he is and it is a true lesson for me. From him, I have learnt to be charitable and generous. Not only he but his family – each and every one of them – is a role model for me. They are generous to a fault, very kind, caring and concerned about all the people around them, and extremely helpful to those in need. I am truly blessed to be a part of uncle's family. I continue to be inspired by all of them and am very thankful to them. There is no better person that I can think of, to write a book on happiness. He is a living example of how to transform one's life to become happy, stress-free, productive, and passionate.

Rey Agard

It is said that a mans life does not consist in the abundance of the things he possessed. This statement describe a person who is selfless and tends to love others more than themselves. A person that cares deeply about others. I honestly declare that Mr Kripalu fits the description. He is one of the most compassionate person I ever met. He has an infectious personality that provides a warm environment for socializing and meaningful debates. You can use all the wonderful adjectives to paint a picture of the glorious and harmonious life of an individual that has an impact on your life, he fits all positives. Space is limited but just to name a few compelling ones. He can be described as affectionate, amiable, charming, vibrant, energetic, friendly, funny, generous, sincere, warm-hearted, passionate, humorous and just full of life. You can truly say when he is around he is the life of the party. It is with a heart of gratitude that I humbly declare I'm honored to know such a man.

Made in the USA
Columbia, SC
26 December 2021